Alexander H.H. Stuart

A Narrative of the Leading Incidents of the Organization of
the First Popular Movement

in Virginia in 1865 to re-establish peaceful relations between the northern

and southern states

Alexander H.H. Stuart

A Narrative of the Leading Incidents of the Organization of the First Popular Movement
in Virginia in 1865 to re-establish peaceful relations between the northern and southern states

ISBN/EAN: 9783337222345

Printed in Europe, USA, Canada, Australia, Japan

Cover: Foto ©ninafisch / pixelio.de

More available books at **www.hansebooks.com**

A NARRATIVE

OF THE

LEADING INCIDENTS OF THE ORGANIZATION

OF THE FIRST

Popular Movement in Virginia

IN 1865

TO

RE-ESTABLISH PEACEFUL RELATIONS BETWEEN THE
NORTHERN AND SOUTHERN STATES, AND OF
THE SUBSEQUENT EFFORTS

OF THE

"Committee of Nine," in 1869,

TO SECURE THE

RESTORATION OF VIRGINIA TO THE UNION,

BY

ALEX. H. H. STUART.

MDCCCLXXXVIII.
WM. ELLIS JONES, BOOK AND JOB PRINTER.
RICHMOND, VA.

A NARRATIVE

OF THE

LEADING INCIDENTS OF THE ORGANIZATION

OF THE FIRST

Popular Movement in Virginia

IN 1865

TO

RE-ESTABLISH PEACEFUL RELATIONS BETWEEN THE
NORTHERN AND SOUTHERN STATES, AND OF
THE SUBSEQUENT EFFORTS

OF THE

'Committee of Nine," in 1869,

TO SECURE THE

RESTORATION OF VIRGINIA TO THE UNION,

BY

ALEX. H. H. STUART.

MDCCCLXXXVIII.
WM. ELLIS JONES, BOOK AND JOB PRINTER.
RICHMOND, VA.

A NARRATIVE.

CHAPTER I.

Several years ago the Virginia Historical Society adopted a resolution, of which the following is a copy :

Resolved, That the Hon. A. H. H. Stuart be requested to prepare for this Society a history of the events of 1869, which led to a restoration of this State to its place in the Union, in which he himself bore so distinguished a part.

An official copy of this resolution was sent to me, to which I replied, expressing my willingness to comply with the request of the Society at as early a day as might be practicable, and at once I proceeded to collect such papers as I thought would be necessary to enable me to do so. But, unfortunately, sickness and other causes compelled me to postpone the fulfillment of my promise to a future day. Time having brought improved health and spirits, I now venture to enter on the performance of the task so long delayed.

In the outset, I wish it to be distinctly understood that I do not propose to write a full history of all that occurred in connection with the "events of 1869" referred to in the resolution of the Society. I have not the material necessary for such a history. Doubtless many things were said and done by others looking to the same end, of which I had no knowledge. All that I propose to do in this paper is to give a narrative of the leading facts and incidents relating to the subject, so far as I was personally connected with or had cognizance of them, accompanied by such papers as may be necessary to verify and explain them.

As I shall speak mainly of matters in which I was an actor or witness, it will readily be conceded that my statement should be made in the first person singular.

But I should feel that my work had been very imperfectly done if I failed, before entering on my narrative of the "events" especially referred to in the resolution of the Society, to refer to others of an antecedent date, which were not less important than the "events of 1869," and which, in fact, opened the way for them.   A knowledge of these facts is necessary to enable the reader to understand the condition of public affairs in 1868–'9.   They supply an important link in the history of Virginia, from the downfall of the Confederacy to the restoration of the State to the Union.   I deem it proper to refer to these events, not only on account of their intrinsic interest as matters of history, but because no permanent record has been made of them, and they are liable to be forgotten, with the men who participated in them.

It will be remembered that it was the practice of General David Hunter, in his raid through Virginia, to destroy all the newspaper offices by breaking up their presses and scattering their type in the streets.   The publication of newspapers was in this way effectually suppressed; and in Staunton, the place of my residence, the only means of printing anything was by an old hand-press, which had escaped the notice of the destroyer, and such type as had been rescued from the gutter into which it had been thrown.   Thus no record of passing events was preserved in files of newspapers, issued from day to day, and the only authentic report of the proceedings of one of the most important popular meetings ever held in Augusta county is to be found in a few copies of an unsightly hand-bill, which was printed on the day after it was held, with the press and type above referred to.

As this meeting set on foot the first organized popular movement for "peace," I cannot doubt that I will render an acceptable service to the public by putting the record of its proceedings in a more enduring form, and placing it under the guardianship of the Virginia Historical Society.

The meeting to which I refer, was a large assemblage of the best people of Augusta county, held at their courthouse in Staunton on 8th of May, 1865, in pursuance of a notice which had been circulated as widely as possible during the preceding week.

The circumstances under which the meeting was held were these: While intelligent and thoughtful men, who were correctly informed as to the exhausted condition of the Confederate treasury, of the absence of supplies of food, clothing, arms, and ammunition necessary to maintain an army in the field, and, above all, of the disparity of numbers and equipment of the troops which were arrayed under the banners of Grant and Lee respectively at the opening of the campaign of 1865, had been forced to the conclusion that the days of the Confederacy were numbered, such was not the belief among the masses of the people in the country.   They had been misled to some extent by the defiant attitude assumed by the Confederate Government, and in larger measure by their unbounded confidence in the abilities of their great leaders, Lee and Johnston, and their associates, which caused them still to cling to the hope of final success.

When, therefore, it became known to the people of Virginia, in April, 1865, that President Davis and his Cabinet and other executive officers of the Confederate Government, and Governor William Smith and the other State officers of Virginia, had been compelled to withdraw from Richmond, and that General Lee had been obliged to evacuate the city and retreat southward with the remnant of his starving army—followed as this news was, in a few days, by intelligence of the surrender of General Lee's army at Appomattox, and the capitulation of General Johnston and his army—the tidings fell on the popular ear like a "fireball in the night," filling the public mind with consternation and dismay !

Men of forecast saw at once that the Confederate cause was lost, and that a continuance of the struggle was hopeless and could result only in a wanton waste of blood and treasure, and an aggravation of the calamities which were inevitable.   They saw, further, that we had been reduced to the sad condition of a people without any government, State or Federal.   The Confederate Government had practically ceased to exist.   The State Government had been overthrown.   The officers of both were refugees, and there was no reasonable prospect of the re-establishment of either.   Every social bond had been ruptured.   Society had been resolved into its original elements.   All laws had become inoperative for want of officers to enforce them.   All the safeguards of life, liberty, and property had been uprooted.   Scenes of lawless violence and rapine were rife in the country.   There were no officials who would be recognized as having authority to represent the people or to give expression to their opinions and wishes.

In a word, a condition of things had arisen in which, if the people wished their voice to be heard, they must speak for themselves !

Such was the state of affairs which existed about the first of May, 1865, when half a dozen or more intelligent gentlemen of Staunton met together, informally, to consider and decide what should be done to meet the emergency which confronted them.   After full and free discussion of the subject in all its aspects, they concluded that the wisest course would be to convoke a mass-meeting of the people of Augusta county, to assemble at their courthouse on Monday, 8th of May, 1865, to decide for themselves.

Notices were accordingly issued, inviting the people to assemble at the time and place above mentioned to give formal expression to their sentiments on the grave questions to be submitted for their consideration. These notices were widely circulated by means of special messengers sent to all parts of the county during the week preceding the day appointed for the meeting; and on Sunday, the day before it was to be held, it naturally became the topic of conversation among the people at their homes, on the highways, and at their respective places of public worship. In this way the purpose to hold the meeting and its objects became known to almost every man in the county, and to many in adjacent counties.

Among those who thus became acquainted with the purpose of the people of Augusta to hold the meeting on the 8th of May, and the subjects to be considered by it, was Governor William Smith. After he had been obliged to leave Richmond, before its formal evacuation, he had sought refuge in a secluded part of Rockbridge county. On learning the facts above stated, and doubtless influenced by a patriotic sense of official duty, he rode to Staunton, a distance of twenty-five miles or more, where he arrived about noon on Sunday, 7th May. Soon after his arrival, he sent invitations to a number of gentlemen who had been most active in getting up the "mass-meeting," requesting them to call on him at his hotel at 3 o'clock P. M. for conference.

I was one of those invited, and at the hour appointed, accompanied by fifteen or twenty other gentlemen, went to the hotel, where we were politely received by the Governor. After the ordinary interchange of salutations and introductions, Governor Smith proceeded to open the interview by referring to the rumors he had heard of the proposed meeting and its objects. Without expressing any opinion, either favorable or unfavorable, to the objects which we had in view, he made known, in decided terms, his opposition to our holding it, on the ground that the proceeding would be irregular, and, to some extent, revolutionary. He referred to the fact that he was the Governor of Virginia, and as such the constitutional representative of the State, and the only person empowered to open negotiations with the Federal authorities to secure peace and the restoration of the State to the Union. He insisted it was not competent for the people of any single county to inaugurate such a movement, thereby ignoring him and his constitutional powers and duties as chief executive officer of the Commonwealth, and therefore urged us to abandon the idea of holding the proposed meeting.

In reply, it was stated that while under a normal condition of public affairs, in which he would be recognized as the lawful Governor of the State of Virginia, his views would be entitled to great weight, yet we thought it was obvious that he who had been a distinguished general in the military service of the Confederate States, and who had been elected Governor of *one of the Confederate States*, under the auspices of the Confederacy, and had taken an oath of allegiance to its government, could not possibly be recognized by the Federal Government as the lawful Governor and constitutional representative of the State of Virginia under the new order of things. Such a recognition would be almost equivalent to a recognition of the Confederate Government itself. All purpose to ignore him or offer him any personal disrespect was earnestly disclaimed; but facts were stubborn things, which could not be ignored. They must be dealt with as they existed. The Confederate Government had collapsed, and there was no reasonable prospect of its ever being re-established. The State Government had been overthrown. We were, therefore, without any government and liable at any time to be overwhelmed by all the horrors of anarchy. We had no representatives who would be recognized as having a right to speak for the people, and hence they must speak for themselves. He was told he was mistaken in supposing that the people of Augusta proposed to act on *behalf of the State*. They claimed no such right. They meant only to give expression to the sentiments and wishes of the county of Augusta, leaving every other county free to take such action as its people might deem proper. The demand for prompt and decided action by the people was urgent. They could not afford to wait for the result of tedious and probably ineffectual diplomatic negotiation, and therefore we must persist in holding the proposed meeting. The conference then closed, without unkind feeling on either side, for each respected the motives of the other, and Governor Smith returned to Rockbridge.

Before dismissing the subject of this interview, it may be proper to say that the sequel proved the soundness of the reasoning of the advocates of the meeting and the fallacy of that of Governor Smith.

The meeting having been held on the 8th of May, and a committee appointed to go to Richmond to confer with the military authorities, it was received with courtesy and attention by the general in command as representing the people. But when Governor Smith shortly afterwards, in his official character, appointed commissioners to negotiate with the military authorities, as soon as these gentlemen presented their credentials they were arrested and held as prisoners, and a reward of $25,000 was offered for the capture of the Governor and the delivery of his person to the officer in command! But, to the honor of our people, it must be added that no one could be tempted, even by such a munificent reward, to play the part of Judas Iscariot!

After the close of the conference with Governor Smith on Sunday afternoon (7th May, 1865), I was notified that it was the wish of the gentlemen who had been most active in getting up the meeting on the 8th that I should preside over its deliberations, and that on taking the chair I should make an address to the people, explaining the objects and purposes of those who called it, with such suggestions as to the policy to be pursued as I might deem appropriate.

After careful consideration, I concluded that in view of the gravity and importance of the questions to be submitted to the meeting, and of the liability of an oral address to be misunderstood and misrepresented, it would be best to commit to writing what I proposed to say. The occasion involved weighty responsibilities. It was proper that the words used should be not only well weighed, but plain and simple, such as could be readily understood by all who might be present. Another fact admonished me of the necessity for caution. A large body of Federal troops occupied the town of Harrisonburg, twenty-five miles distant, and I felt confident that a number of their enterprising "Jesse Scouts" would be present as vigilant spectators and reporters of the proceedings of the meeting. I therefore wrote in advance the address which I proposed to make.

At an early hour on the 8th of May, the people began to assemble in the streets and public grounds near the courthouse to interchange opinions and discuss the great questions which they had been invited to consider and decide. Their solemn countenances and earnest demeanor indicated that they clearly understood and appreciated the gravity of the situation.

Before the hour of 12 M., which had been appointed for the organization of the meeting, a great crowd had assembled in the courthouse, which embodied a large share of the intelligence, patriotism and property of the county. It was in all respects a *representative meeting*, and therefore entitled to give authentic expression to the sentiments and wishes of the people of the county.

Punctually at 12 o'clock the meeting was called to order, and the chairman and secretaries nominated and elected.

Having been chosen as chairman, after a brief explanation of the reasons which had induced me to reduce to writing the address which I was about to make to the meeting, I proceeded to *read it from the manuscript*, which I did slowly and distinctly so that every word could be heard and understood by the large and attentive audience. After it had thus been read, at the request of the secretaries I delivered the manuscript to them to be incorporated into their report of the proceedings. These proceedings were faithfully and accurately recorded by the secretaries, and as there was no newspaper published in Staunton at that time, they were printed on the following day in hand-bills on the little hand-press, to which I have already referred, and many copies were sent to representative men in other counties. A copy of that hand-bill is now before me, and will be annexed to this narrative. It is in the following words :

MASS-MEETING OF THE PEOPLE OF AUGUSTA !

In pursuance of a public notice, which had been extensively circulated, a large and respectable meeting of the people of Augusta county assembled at the courthouse on Monday, 8th of May, "to take measures looking to a reorganization of the government of Virginia in conformity to the Constitution and laws of the United States."

On motion of Colonel Wm. A. Bell, Hon. ALEX. H. H. STUART was called to the chair and Dr. THOS. W. SHELTON and W. H. H. LYNN were appointed secretaries.

On taking the chair, Mr. Stuart spoke substantially as follows:

Fellow Citizens:—We have met together to-day to decide what course we ought to pursue under the peculiar circumstances by which we are surrounded.

The war which has raged throughout our land for four years past, and has left so many evidences of its desolating power in every part of it, has at length ceased. The veteran armies of Lee and Johnston have capitulated and a similar fate doubtless awaits, if it has not already befallen, the Confederate forces west of the Mississippi. The President of the Confederate States and his Cabinet have been constrained to abandon the seat of government, without any reasonable prospect of being able to re-establish themselves and resume the exercise of their functions in any of the Southern States.

The Governor of Virginia has also withdrawn himself from the capitol, taking with him most of the principal officers of the State Government.

There has thus been a virtual abdication of the Confederate Government and a suspension of the functions of the authorities of the State.

In this anomalous condition of things, when those officers who were

•

chosen to represent the people and to be the guardians of their rights and interests have lost the power to do so, it becomes the duty of the people to speak for themselves, and to determine what measures may be best for the advancement of their safety and welfare.

All must admit that the war is ended, and that there is no purpose to resume military operations. The recent surrenders of Generals Lee and Johnston embraced much the larger number of the experienced and skilful officers of the Southern army, and the articles of capitulation and arrangements subsequently entered into have placed almost the entire organized military force east of the Mississippi under obligations not to take up arms against the United States until regularly exchanged.

We are thus in the extraordinary condition of a people deprived of the benefit of any regular government, either civil or military. The tendency of such a state of things is to disorder and anarchy In some instances marauding parties of armed men have plundered our citizens and acts of violence have been committed, which are calculated to create a sense of insecurity amongst our people.

Under these circumstances, we are assembled to consider what course we shall adopt to secure the best protection of person and property and the largest measure of our rights, both personal and political, which may be practicable.

It has been suggested that our wisest course is to do nothing, but to await the development of events. I do not approve this suggestion. I think we should endeavor as far as we can to give shape and direction to our own destiny. If we fail, we will at least save ourselves the reproach of not having made an effort to do so. Those who advocate a policy merely passive, seem to act on the idea that we have lost all our rights and must accept such form of government as may be imposed on us. This notion arises from the fact that those who entertain it confound the ideas of POWER and RIGHT, which are two very different things. A victorious party may have the power to impose an obnoxious form of government on its defeated adversary, but it by no means follows that it has the right to do so.

In my judgment, it is proper that the people of Virginia should express in public meetings—the only mode left to them of giving authentic expression to their sentiments—their recognition of the fact that the war has ceased, finally ceased; that the attempted revolution has finally failed, and that there is no purpose on their part to renew it.

When it is thus made manifest that the people accept the fate, which in the fortunes of war has befallen them, that the war is over and that they are prepared to recognize the authority of the Constitution of the United States, from that moment our relations to the United States Government are materially modified, and rights which may have remained in abeyance during the continuance of hostilities are immediately revived in full force and vigor.

When the war is at an end, all those powers claimed as war powers and as matters of military necessity must cease with it.

The restoration of peace will bring up for discussion and decision many novel and complicated questions. The experience and the precedents derived from the history of other nations will furnish very insufficient guides in their solution, because the history of the world affords no case that is parallel to ours. In other countries the relation of the citizen or subject to his government is simple and direct. He owes allegiance to but one government—under our complex system every citizen owes allegiance to two governments. Before the war every citizen owed allegiance to his State as well as to the United States. He was bound to defend both. It was thus a double or a divided allegiance with the line of demarcation not very distinctly defined. When, therefore, a conflict occurred it was not always easy to determine the path of duty or safe to pursue it, for what was obedience to the one might be treason against the other.

The war having terminated and the Confederate government having potentially ceased to exist, we are released from all claim of allegiance to it and remitted to our rights as citizens of Virginia. What may be the extent of those rights, or how far any individual may have forfeited his rights, may be a question to be determined hereafter in the mode prescribed by the Constitution of the United States. One thing, however, we may safely assume. A State in its political capacity cannot commit treason. A State as a political community cannot incur forfeitures. Treason can only be committed by individuals, and the penalties can be inflicted on individuals only. How far a State can throw the ægis of her protection over her citizens who acted under her authority will have to be settled hereafter.

I take it, therefore, that Virginia still has rights under the Constitution of the United States, which have only been suspended during the abortive effort to sever her connection with the United States, and it seems to me to be our duty to try and have those rights recognized and respected.

If it be true, as has been almost universally assumed in the Northern States, that the ordinances of secession were mere nullities and absolutely void, then the Southern States have never severed their connection with the United States—have never been out of the Union, and are therefore entitled, from the moment the war ceases, to resume their position as members of the Union.

I advert to these questions with no view to discuss them, but simply to combat the idea that all our rights have been lost and as a satisfactory reason for meeting promptly the issue which has been forced upon us, and declaring that so far as we are concerned (and we believe we speak the sentiments of Virginia) the war has finally closed; that we have no purpose to renew it; that we are prepared to conform our State government to the changed condition of public affairs; and that we are convinced that by a wise and conciliatory policy on the part of the Federal authorities, peace and tranquility can soon be firmly and permanently re-established.

After the close of Mr. Stuart's remarks, on motion of Hugh W. Sheffey, Esq., the chair was instructed to appoint a committee of thirteen to prepare and report suitable resolutions for the consideration of the meeting.

The chair thereupon named the following gentlemen to constitute the committee.

H. W. Sheffey, T. J. Michie, Jno. B. Baldwin, W. M. Tate, D. S. Bell, J. M. McCue, M. G. Harman, H. G. Guthrie, Chesley Kinney, Bolivar Christian, George Baylor, Absalom Coiner, J. Givens Fulton.

After some time spent in deliberation, the committee reported the following series of resolutions:

RESOLUTIONS.

1. *Resolved*, That we believe we express the thorough conviction of the people of Augusta county, when we declare that opposition to the authority of the United States within this county is at an end and that there is no purpose on the part of any of our people to attempt any renewal of it.

2. *Resolved*, That the people of Augusta county, recognizing the necessity of reorganizing the government of Virginia so as to conform to the Constitution and laws of the United States, are prepared to co-operate in good faith with the people of other portions of the State for that purpose.

3. *Resolved*, That in our opinion the best mode of effecting the object proposed is by a State Convention, chosen by the voters and organized upon the basis of the House of Delegates.

4. *Resolved*, That a committee of five be appointed to go to Richmond and ascertain whether the military authorities of the United States will interpose any obstruction to the election, assembling and action of such a convention for the purpose indicated, and that the chairman of this meeting be the chairman of said committee.

5. *Resolved*, That this committee be also authorized to confer with similar committees to be appointed in other counties, and to adopt in concert such measures as will best promote the objects herein declared.

In pursuance of the request of the committee, Hon. John B. Baldwin proceeded to explain the nature and purport of the resolutions and to urge their adoption in a speech of great power and eloquence, which produced a profound impression on the audience.

After the close of Colonel Baldwin's speech, no other person manifesting any desire to speak, the resolutions were again read to the meeting *seriatim*, and each resolution adopted by a unanimous vote.

After the other resolutions had been adopted, on motion of Bolivar Christian, Esq., the chairman was instructed to appoint at his leisure the members of the committee contemplated by the fourth resolution.

The proceedings of the meeting were marked by great solemnity and dignity, and evidently expressed the deliberate sense of the people of Augusta. The assembly was a full one, and embraced a large share of the intelligence and weight of the county.

ALEX. H. H. STUART, *Chairman.*

THOS. W. SHELTON, } *Secretaries.*
WM. H. H. LYNN,

I have nothing to add to the record made by the secretaries of the proceedings of this meeting. It is in all respects full and accurate.

It will be observed that the fourth resolution provided for the " appointment of a committee of five, of which the chairman of the meeting shall be chairman, to go to Richmond and ascertain whether the military authorities of the United States will interpose any objection to the election and assembling of a State Convention chosen on the basis of the House of Delegates "

By a subsequent resolution "the chairman was instructed to appoint, at his leisure, the other members of the committee contemplated by the fourth resolution."

Under the power thus conferred on me, I appointed as my associates on the committee, Judge Hugh W. Sheffey, Colonel John B. Baldwin, Colonel Michael G. Harman, and Major William M. Tate.

A few days afterwards the committee went to Richmond and sought an interview with the military authorities. We were courteously received, but were informed that the officer in command had no authority to consider or decide the questions which were the subjects of our mission. We were also informed that Hon. Francis H. Peirpoint had been recognized by the United States Government as Governor of Virginia, and that in a few days he would be in Richmond to enter on the discharge of his duties ; and it was suggested that we had better await his arrival and make our communication to him. We accordingly remained in Richmond until Governor Peirpoint had been duly installed as Governor under military auspices. We then called on him and exhibited to him a copy of the resolutions which had been adopted by the people of Augusta, and explained fully the objects of our mission. A full and free discussion of all the questions connected with the restoration of Virginia to the Union ensued, the details of which it is not necessary to state. The Governor, throughout the conference, displayed an amicable and patriotic spirit, and closed the interview by giving such assurances of sympathy and friendly co-operation as were satisfactory to the committee, and thus their mission closed.

It is proper to add that, during the sojourn of the committee in Richmond, we were met by delegates from other counties, whose people, having heard of the action taken by the people of Augusta, had hastened to hold similar meetings and select committees to co-operate with us.

We also learned from the newspapers that the people of counties and cities of other Southern States were making movements of a similar character and with the same end in view.

It will thus be seen *that the first organized popular movement for peace and the restoration of Virginia to the Federal Union was made by the people of Augusta* in their great mass-meeting, on the 8th of May, 1865.

Results proved that the meeting was not only a bold but a wise and judicious movement. It dispelled many popular delusions caused by the over-confidence of the Confederate authorities. It uncovered the nakedness of the Confederate cause. It awakened public thought and gave a new direction to public opinion. It illustrated the genius of our institutions by a majestic exhibition of popular sovereignty. When politicians faltered and were at a loss what course to take, the people quietly took the reins of government from their hands and acted for themselves. Under their guidance hostilities ceased and social order was re-established. And thus the extraordinary spectacle was presented to the world of a fierce and bloody war of four years' duration being substantially closed by the direct action of the people themselves, without the intervention of any of the forms of diplomacy. And there is good reason to believe that but for the atrocious murder of President Lincoln, and the exasperated feeling caused by it, the terms of permanent and satisfactory peace could have been adjusted at an early day. That deplorable event, and the subsequent quarrels between Congress and President Johnson, rendered it impossible to make any further movement for restoration during his ill-starred administration.

It may be fairly inferred from the following letter, which was addressed to me by Governor William Smith, dated 27th of February, 1880, that in the light of subsequent events he had seen cause to change his opinion as to the wisdom of the meeting of the people of Augusta on the 8th of May, 1865. He wrote as follows :

WARRENTON, *February 27, 1880.*

Hon. A. H. H. STUART :

My Dear Sir,—I have your very satisfactory favor of the 25th instant, but am sorry to have again to trouble you, but I should be very glad to have a copy of the proceedings of your meeting of the 8th of May, 1865, as I may wish to publish it.

When I left Richmond the night of 2d of April, 1865, it was with the firm resolve to do everything in my power still to change the current of our disasters. With that view, I declined President Davis's invitation to accompany him the night of the evacuation. With that view, I ordered the Capitol officers, the Public Guard, and the State Cadets to report to me in Lynchburg, etc. And when they failed to do so, it was with this view that I followed President Davis to Greensboro, North Carolina, to obtain from him a transfer to me of all his authority, etc., in Virginia. And when, most strangely, after a full explanation of my plans and purposes, he refused my request, it was still with the same view, desperate as was the prospect, that I felt it to be my duty to collect public sentiment in every way I could, traveling many a weary mile, and finally reaching your town on the 7th May, 1865, the time you state, and no doubt correctly, to know if the people were willing, in any form, to prosecute the war or quietly submit. I soon inferred from what passed during the evening I was with you and friends that your great county was hopeless, and that all further struggles were useless, etc. Now, I want your proceedings of the next day, because they were the first embodiment of such sentiments by so important a portion of the people, etc.

I shall be glad to get your educational report.

Yours very truly,

WILLIAM SMITH.

This closes my narrative of the events of 1865. It shows what had been done toward restoration. The war had ceased, and the rights of person and property were comparatively safe. Anarchy had been averted. But much still remained to be done to secure the full measure of the civil and political rights of Virginia as one of the members of the Federal Union. The time for action on this subject, however, had not yet come. Prudence admonished the people to wait patiently, to watch vigilantly the development of events, and to seize promptly and boldly the first opportunity for action that offered a chance of success. All knew that while a great and good work had been done in re-establishing peace and social order, a much more important one—the restoration of Virginia to her rights in the Union—remained to be accomplished at a later day.

The foregoing narrative may properly be regarded as the first chapter in the history of the efforts of Virginia to accomplish her restoration to her position and rights in the Union.

CHAPTER II.

I proceed now to give a narrative of subsequent events, so far as I was an active participator in or a vigilant observer of them. This will be more directly responsive to the resolution of the Virginia Historical Society, and may be called the second chapter.

It would be foreign to the purposes of this paper to refer to all the important events which marked the progress of Virginia from 1865 to 1868. They belong to the general history of the Commonwealth, and are as well known to the public as to myself.

It is sufficient for my purpose to advert to a few of them, which have a direct relation to the subject of this narrative.

In 1865, after Peirpoint had been installed as Governor of Virginia, elections of members of the Senate and House of Delegates of Virginia and of members of the House of Representatives of the United States were ordered, with the sanction of President Andrew Johnson. At this Congressional election I was chosen to represent the district in which I resided in the House of Representatives of the United States.

On the day appointed for the commencement of the session of Congress, the Representatives who had been elected by the Southern States, after seeing that their certificates of election were in due form and properly authenticated and filed in the office of the clerk of the House of Representatives, took their seats in the hall. But on the formal roll-call, preliminary to the administration of the oath of office to members, it was found that the clerk *had failed to enter the name of any Southern member on it.* By what authority this outrage on the constitutional rights of the Southern members was perpetrated I do not know. That it was in violation of the Constitution, is obvious from the fact that the *Constitution itself specifically enumerates and defines* the requisites for eligibility of members, and Congress has no constitutional power to add to or take from, to enlarge or curtail, qualifications thus fixed by the Constitution itself. We were not permitted to be heard in defence of our rights, and by this lawless device we were quietly evicted from our seats! That this act was a gross usurpation of power, not warranted by the Constitution, was at a later day substantially admitted by leading members of Congress, when they acknowledged that they had been *acting outside the limits of the Constitution!*

I refer to this fact as one which tended largely to retard the growth of fraternal feeling between the Northern and Southern people and to reopen the wounds of the war, which, under the soothing influences of time, had begun to heal.

It is also necessary to state that provision had been made by the military authorities of "District No. 1" (as Virginia was then called) for the election, in October, 1867, of members of a convention to frame a new Constitution for the State. It was provided that this convention should assemble in Richmond on the 3d of December, 1867; but there were such stringent restrictions imposed on eligibility of members that much the larger number of the men of intelligence, education, and experience in public affairs were effectually excluded from participation in its deliberations.

The convention was mainly composed of ignorant and excited negroes, led by greedy adventurers from the North, popularly known as "carpet-baggers," and a few recreant natives, who were designated "scallawags." To this hideous majority were opposed a small minority of the better class of citizens, generally young men, who, not having held any public office before the war, were not disfranchised by the Congressional iron-clad test oath.

These young men fought a good fight in defence of the rights and interests of the people of Virginia, but found themselves powerless to resist the torrent of malignity and radicalism which swept everything before it.

The convention remained in session from 3d December, 1867, to the 24th April, 1868.

The result of the labors of such a body of men could readily be anticipated. It was the formation and recommendation of a Constitution at war with every principle of civil liberty, bristling with test oaths and disfranchisements and other enormities, and containing provisions artfully and insidiously worded, so as not only to throw the whole political power of the State into the hands of the most ignorant classes of her people, but to render practicable the virtual confiscation, by the agency of corrupt judges and ignorant and prejudiced and interested juries, of the estate of every one who had ever been a slaveholder! Under this Constitution it was provided that no man who could not take the Congressional test oath could be allowed *to vote* at any public election, or *be eligible to any public office*, or be allowed *to serve on any jury!* Fortunately, the act of Congress, which allowed the convention to be held, provided that the Constitution which it might form should be reported to Congress for its approval before it could be submitted to popular vote for ratification or rejection.

The publication of this monstrous document filled the public mind with horror and dismay. The only rational hope of defeating its adoption, lay in an effort to induce Congress to withhold its approval. But, as Virginia was then without representation in Congress, she had no accredited agent whose duty and privilege it would be to expose its enormities and demand its modification or rejection. Although this fact was well known to every man of ordinary intelligence, when the Constitution was transmitted to Congress

2

for approval or disapproval, not a voice was heard from Virginia in the way of protest or objection. Everybody remained quiescent, either in the belief that "what was everybody's business was nobody's business," or in the delusive hope that some Northern member of Congress would volunteer to examine, critically, the voluminous instrument and point out the grounds of objection to it. I remember when, at a later day, I was in Washington, I met Mr. James Brooks, of New York, then a leading Conservative member of the House of Representatives, and inquired of him how it happened that such a monstrous instrument could have received the approval of the House? His reply was, that very few members knew anything about it. It was reported to the House by the appropriate committee as the work of a convention of Virginia, and as no one from Virginia had even suggested an objection to it, it was presumed to be satisfactory to everybody, and passed as a matter of course. He closed by the pertinent inquiry, "If the people of Virginia will not attend to their own interests, how can they expect other people to do so for them?"

I was a vigilant observer of the progress of events at Washington, and had written to a friend in Richmond, urging him to call on one of the organized political committees in that city and get them to *formulate a protest* against the approval of the Constitution by the House of Representatives. His reply was, that he had done so, and that the answer was that the committees thought they had no jurisdiction over the subject, and declined to take any action in the matter.

It thus happened that by default of the people of Virginia, the bill approving the proposed Constitution of Virginia (popularly called the Underwood Constitution) was allowed to pass the House of Representatives, and be sent to the Senate for its concurrence, without a whisper of opposition!

Shortly thereafter, Congress passed a joint resolution for the usual Christmas recess, to commence about the 21st of December, 1868, and to continue to the 4th of January, 1869. This action gave us a respite of about a fortnight, as it was hardly probable the Senate would act on the bill before the commencement of the recess. I have not access to the journals of Congress, and therefore I cannot give with certainty the dates of either of these events.

It was evident that unless some measure was adopted within the ensuing fortnight to arrest the passage of the bill by the Senate, the Underwood Constitution would be permanently fastened on Virginia.

I had looked in vain to the Richmond press for some movement to organize opposition to its passage. But apathy seemed to pervade the State, and everybody remained quiescent. Thus the strange spectacle was presented to the country of a high-spirited people, who in 1861 had promptly rushed to arms to encounter all the dangers and horrors of civil war, in defence of their rights against a remote and contingent danger, yet now, when a disaster tenfold greater in degree, actually present and certain, was immediately impending, failed to raise voice or arm to ward off the unspeakable calamity!

I have no doubt that hundreds—nay, thousands—of my fellow-citizens thought and felt as I did as to the necessity of taking action on the subject. But no one seemed to be willing to assume the responsibility of taking the lead!

Under these circumstances, as the necessity for moving in the matter was urgent, and the time within which action likely to lead to a successful result was limited to two weeks, I determined to sound a note of alarm by calling the attention of the people of Virginia to the frightful dangers which threatened them, and urging those who thought as I did to unite in an organized attempt to avert them.

With this object in view, I wrote "a communication," over the signature "Senex," intended for publication in the Richmond *Dispatch*. This paper was written entirely on my own responsibility, and without conference or consultation with any one. My purpose was to try and arouse the people to the necessity of immediate action, and to suggest as the most feasible, if not the *only*, means of obtaining relief from the disfranchisements and test oaths embodied in the Underwood Constitution, the tender to Congress on behalf of Virginia of a compromise, on the basis of *universal suffrage* as an equivalent for *universal amnesty*.

After the close of the Presidential and Congressional elections of November, 1868, it became manifest to all thoughtful men that *universal suffrage* was a foregone conclusion in the Northern mind. It was as inevitable as any decree of fate. The Northern States had the political as well as the physical power to enforce it. Nor had they left any doubt as to their fixed purpose to exercise that power, for they had incorporated it as a cardinal feature of the future policy of the Republican party.

If, therefore, we could secure as an equivalent for it relief from the disfranchisements and test oaths, which would make slaves of us for a generation to come, it would be so much substantial gain for a merely nominal concession !

I knew full well, however, that in the condition of public opinion which then existed in Virginia, in regard to granting the right of suffrage to the ignorant negroes, the simple announcement of the proposed basis of compromise would arouse a storm of fierce indignation throughout the State, and draw down on him who had the hardihood to suggest it a torrent of denunciation and obloquy which few men have been called on to endure !

The sequel proved that I was not mistaken in this respect. The people were not prepared to reason calmly on the subject. The sacrifice they were required to make was hateful to them. For a time, passion and prejudice exercised unlimited sway over the popular mind, and no inconsiderable portion of the public press. Six months elapsed before the sober reason and common sense of the people enabled them to look at the other side of the question, and to comprehend the incalculable advantages which they had secured to themselves by yielding gracefully to what was inevitable !

The article, "Senex," was in the following words:

To the Editors of the Dispatch :

The present unhappy condition of Virginia, and the gloomy prospects which seem to lie before us, naturally fill every thoughtful mind with painful apprehension. Should the Constitution recommended by the recent convention be ratified, or be reported to Congress as ratified by the popular vote, the condition of the Commonwealth will be simply intolerable. Almost every man worthy of public trust will be disfranchised, not only as to office, but in regard to suffrage ; and the political power of the State will pass into the hands of strangers and adventurers. The property of the country will be at the mercy of those who pay little or no portion of the taxes, and we shall be plundered at the will of those who come among us to obtain office and gratify their greed for spoils.

It requires much prudence on the part of the people of Virginia, and the sacrifice of many cherished opinions, to avert these direful calamities. The question is now forced upon us to decide, not what we would desire—not what we are willing to take—but what we shall be allowed to retain.

We have already made many and painful sacrifices. We have sanctioned by our votes the constitutional amendment which abolished slavery, and we have shaped our legislation so as to accord with the provisions of that amendment.

These measures were exceedingly distasteful to most of our people, and many thought at the time they would be fatal to the prosperity of the State. But in large portions of the Commonwealth, if not throughout its whole extent, it has been found that the results have not been so disastrous

as was anticipated. In some districts, in which there was not an over proportion of blacks, the change has proved beneficial; and the writer of this
paper has heard many who had been slaveholders say that they would be
unwilling to restore slavery if it were in their power to do so. As immigration flows into the State, this opinion will become more general, and when
our political troubles are finally settled, it will prove to be almost universal.

But the point to which I now wish to draw public attention is, what further sacrifices of opinions and prejudices are necessary to render those
which we have already made productive of good fruit, and to secure to ourselves and our families exemption from the evils to which I have adverted?
As matters now stand, we have great reason to apprehend that the ballot-
boxes will be so manipulated at the coming election as to fasten the proposed Constitution, with all its odious features of disfranchisement and
burdensome taxation, upon us. We are naturally led, then, to inquire,
how can this bitter cup be turned away from our lips?

There is one point on which Northern sentiment, or, as the politicians
and the press of the North are pleased to call it, "the national will," seems
to be fixed and irreversible; and that is, that universal suffrage, without
distinction of race or color, shall be forced on us. They maintain that
negro suffrage is a legitimate, "if not a necessary sequence" of negro
emancipation. Judge Chase and the more conservative Republicans hold
this opinion, and urge us to adopt it as the means of avoiding greater evils.
This proposition is exceedingly unpalatable to the people of the South.
We know that the negroes are not qualified to exercise the elective franchise, and that they would be unsafe depositaries of political power. But
how are we to help ourselves? We are powerless to resist by arms, and the
recent national elections have shown that we are equally powerless at the
ballot-box.

There is an old adage that "half a loaf is better than no bread," and I
would respectfully ask, is not ours a case for the application of that proposition? Is it not better to surrender *half* than to lose *all?* Is it not better
to take universal suffrage, with an exemption from disfranchisement and
the other evils to which I have alluded, than to have them all forced upon
us? After grievous travail of spirit, I have come to the conclusion that
such is the dictate of prudence and common sense.

The Southern mind is naturally sensitive in regard to everything like
negro equality. We cannot forget that they were recently our slaves, nor
can we dismiss from our minds the conviction that they are naturally inferior to the white race, and the knowledge that they are uneducated and
ignorant of the first principles of government. Every step, therefore, in
the direction of that equality has been taken reluctantly and with many
misgivings. When it was proposed to introduce negroes as witnesses, the
public mind of Virginia was not prepared for the proposition. At first, their
admissibility was limited by law to cases in which a negro was a party.
Afterwards the restriction was removed, and they became lawful, competent
witnesses in all cases, and, as far as I have heard, no mischief has resulted.
Their testimony is received and weighed like that of other men. But
competency does not necessarily imply credibility. Their testimony is

believed or disbelieved in proportion to the character of the witness and the intrinsic probability of his evidence.

We now look with extreme aversion on negro suffrage. It is natural we should do so for reasons already stated. But may we not find upon actual experiment, as in the case of negro testimony, that it is not such a bad thing as we have been accustomed to believe?

The inherent inferiority of the race, and their want of education and property, will necessarily place them in a position of subordination to the superior race. This has been found to be the case in Mississippi, Georgia and Louisiana. Knowledge is power. Property is power. Would it not, therefore, be strange if the superior intelligence and accumulated property of the superior race should not exercise a controlling influence over the ignorance and penury of the inferior? It seems to me a contrary apprehension must be ill-founded, because it is opposed to reason and human experience.

Will it not, therefore, be wise for the people of Virginia to make up their minds to come up at once to the proposition of Judge Chase and the New York *Tribune*—"Universal suffrage and universal amnesty"? Better that than "*universal suffrage and universal disfranchisement.*"

Matters may not work altogether smoothly for a time. We may have some trouble in portions of the State, but it will be temporary. The influx of whites from abroad, and the efflux of blacks from the State, will soon establish Caucasian preponderance on a firm basis.

What we want is peace. We want these troublesome questions settled, so that the tide of immigration may flow into Virginia. As long as we are in our present abnormal condition immigrants will not come among us, because they do not know what to expect in the future. Let these questions be settled—it matters not how—and population and capital will flow in an unbroken stream into all parts of our State, building up our cities, opening our mines, buying and improving our land, constructing new railways and canals, and giving vigor and activity to our industrial interests.

Thousands are now anxiously awaiting this settlement. Let us throw no farther obstacles in the way. Let us say to the conservative Republicans, we accede to your proposition. Let us respond to General Grant's demand for peace. When peace is restored, and the Southern States are again represented in Congress by men who will truly reflect their sentiments, we can have a word to say in regard to the future policy of the country. It seems to me obvious that by this course we must gain something, and cannot lose anything.

And now for the mode of carrying these ideas into practical effect. This is a subject by no means free from difficulty, and the time for action is short. We cannot get up another convention to form a new Constitution. But a Constitution derives its validity, not from the body which frames and proposes it, but from its ratification by the votes of the people. If the Legislature of a State were to instruct the Court of Appeals, instead of a convention, to frame a Constitution to be voted on by the people, it would be competent for them to do so; and such a Constitution, if ratified by the popular vote, would be just as valid and obligatory as if the same had been framed by a convention assembled in the usual form.

To avoid unnecessary delay, let the Executive Committee, in the interval between the present time and the 1st of February, take the Constitution of 1850 and the proposed Constitution of 1861, and from the two select the better provisions, omitting the word "white" and all other provisions that would be in conflict with "universal suffrage and universal amnesty," and thus frame a complete Constitution.

Let us, then, avail ourselves of this idea. Let the Central Conservative Committee call together, say two gentlemen of approved wisdom and integrity from each Congressional district, to meet that committee in Richmond about the first of February, to agree upon a Constitution for Virginia, to be submitted to Congress as a substitute for that recommended by the late convention. Let this Constitution embody the universal suffrage and universal amnesty proposition in its broadest terms, and negro eligibility to boot!

On the 1st of February the Executive Committee and their adjunct advisers could come together, and, by limiting discussion to five minutes on each proposition, they could revise the work of the committee and perfect a Constitution in three or four days to be presented to Congress as a substitute for the Constitution which has already elicited such strong censure from the New York *Times* and other Northern papers.

May I ask, Mr. Editor, that you will give this proposition your calm consideration, and, if you approve, that you will extend to it the support of your vigorous pen and invoke the aid of the press of the State?

It seems to me that this will be the easiest and the shortest way of getting out of our present unhappy difficulties.

SENEX.

This article, "Senex," was written on the evening of 19th December, 1868, and was not finished until 11 o'clock at night. As the mail left Staunton for Richmond at a very early hour next morning, I apprehended some difficulty in having it mailed in time for the first train. Being anxious to have it published as promptly as practicable, so as to afford as much time as possible to the people to consider a question of so much gravity and importance, I enclosed it in an unsealed envelope, directed to "The Editors of the *Dispatch*," and at sunrise next morning carried it to the railroad station, intending to mail it on the train, unless I could find some person going to Richmond, to whom I could safely entrust it for delivery to the *Dispatch*, with an earnest request for its publication.

Fortunately, I found my friend General John Echols on the platform, about to take the train for Richmond. I then explained to him the object of my early visit, and delivered to him the envelope, telling him that it contained "a communication" to the *Dispatch* on a subject of a momentous character, which I wished to have published as promptly as possible. I added that I did not know what he might think of it, but that I hoped he would approve it, and at the proper time would unite with me in carrying it into effect. I begged him, when he took his seat on the cars, to read it carefully and give me his aid in securing its prompt publication, which he promised to do. My hope was that it would be published in the *Dispatch* of Tuesday, the 21st of December, 1868, or in any event on Wednesday, 22d. I also said to General Echols that if any enquiry were made why I did not attach *my own name to it, and thereby assume the responsibility of its authorship*, I authorized him to say, on my behalf, that I was restrained from doing so solely by the consideration that I feared some persons might think me guilty of vanity in assuming that my name would add anything to the intrinsic weight of the sentiments expressed in the communication. But, if the editors desired to indicate who was *the responsible author of it*, they were at liberty to refer to me in any way they might think proper as bearing that relation to it. The General then took his departure on the train, carrying the paper with him.

The communication not having appeared in the *Dispatch* of Tuesday or Wednesday, I naturally inferred that there was an unwillingness on the part of the editors to publish it at all.

General Echols returned to Staunton by the night train of Wednesday, the 23d. When I met him next morning he informed me that he had read my " communication " with much interest, and, cordially approving it, he had taken the liberty of reading it to several friends whom he met on the train, who also approved it. When he arrived at the Exchange Hotel, he was gratified to find that Colonel W. T. Sutherlin, of Danville, was one of the guests. Having confidence in his good sense and sound judgment, he sought an early opportunity to read to him my paper and invite his co-operation in the movement proposed, which Colonel Sutherlin promptly promised to give. The paper was then taken by General Echols to the editors of the *Dispatch*, who, after reading it, made some objection to publishing it in their paper, on the ground that public opinion was not prepared to entertain the propositions contained in it, and asked why I had not signed my name to it? In reply to this inquiry, General Echols stated the reasons which had restrained me from signing it, but informed him that I was willing that the editors *should refer to me as the author* of the communication and *responsible for its contents.*

To this proposition no definite answer was given, and the objections of the editor did not seem to be removed by it. Being thus discouraged, General Echols took the communication to the office of the *Whig* for publication, but was met with similar objections to those made at the office of the *Dispatch*, and a like answer was given to the enquiry, why I had not signed my name to the paper. The result was a polite refusal to publish it. It was then submitted to the editor of the *Enquirer*, who at once, and emphatically, declined to publish it under any circumstances. On his return to the hotel, General Echols reported the result of his mission to Colonel Sutherlin, who readily volunteered to go with him, after supper, to see Mr. Alexander Mosely, then editor of the *Whig*, at his private residence and try to overcome his objections to publishing the communication. They accordingly went to Mr. Mosely's, and had an interview with him, in which, after some discussion, it was finally agreed that Mr. Mosely would publish it in the *Whig* on three conditions : 1st, that I should be referred to as the author ; 2d, that the editor should not be held committed to support the propositions contained inthe paper ; and 3d, that the *Dispatch* should agree to publish it simultaneously under like conditions.*

The *Dispatch* having consented to this arrangement, the publication was made in both papers on the 25th of December, 1868, indicating me, unmistakably, as the author.

After my communication had been sent to Richmond, as above stated, and while the publication of it was in suspense, I held conferences with several leading citizens of Staunton, informing them of the contents of the paper I had written, and urging them to unite with me in organizing opposition to the passage by the Senate of the bill which had been sent to it by the House of Representatives.

Among the most prominent were Thomas J. Michie, Esq., Judge H. W. Sheffey, Nicholas K. Trout, Esq., Major H. M. Bell, R. H. Catlet, and others. Colonel John B. Baldwin, who always took an active part in all matters affecting public affairs, was at that time in Washington attending to professional business in the Supreme Court of the United States, and therefore I could not consult with him.

---

* The foregoing statements as to the publication of the article, "Senex," was submitted to General John Echols, who writes, 10th December, 1887, to the author : "I think that you have stated, at least with substantial accuracy, the manner in which the article, 'Senex,' came to be published, and the connection which I, as your friend and agent, had therewith."

On Friday, the 25th of December, 1868, these gentlemen met by appointment at my office in Staunton, for the purpose of considering the best means of promoting the object we had in view. General Echols and Colonel John B. Baldwin (who had meanwhile returned to Staunton) were also present at that meeting. The whole subject was fully discussed and considered in all its bearings, and all concurred in the necessity of securing the co-operation of gentlemen of intelligence and weight of character in all parts of the State. All felt that the necessity for action was urgent, as the time for taking it (little more than a fortnight) was very limited. We therefore agreed *forthwith* to issue invitations to prominent gentlemen in all parts of the State to meet us in Richmond on 31st of December, 1868, to confer and decide what measures should be adopted to rescue the State from the dangers which threatened her. The form of the invitation was then prepared, and the names of all the gentlemen present were attached to it, with the exception of that of Judge Sheffey, which (though he was in full accord with us and willing to sign it), we thought had better be omitted, as he then occupied the position of judge of our Circuit Court. The paper was, without delay, sent to the office of the *Spectator* to be printed. In a short time the work was executed, and more than a hundred copies were returned to us. These were promptly placed in envelopes, directed and mailed to leading men, who we thought would probably be disposed to co-operate with us.

On the 30th of December, Mr. T. J. Michie, General Echols, Major H. M. Bell, N. K. Trout, and myself, went to Richmond to attend the meeting. Colonel J. B. Baldwin did not accompany us, partly, as I believed, from the urgency of professional business which had accumulated in his office during his absence at Washington, and partly because of doubts which had arisen in his mind whether public opinion was prepared to entertain so bold a proposition.

We were met in Richmond by a number of the gentlemen who had been invited to join us in conference, and by a number of others to whom formal invitations had not been sent, but who had heard of and sympathized with the objects of the meeting, and others who were attracted by curiosity to know what we proposed to do. The whole subject, in all its aspects, was the subject of earnest conversation in the halls and public rooms of the hotel during the evening of our arrival and the forenoon of the following day.

Colonel Carrington, the proprietor of the Exchange Hotel, having kindly tendered us the use of a large room in his hotel, known as the

"Concert Hall," for our meetings, we assembled in it at noon on 31st of December, 1868. An organization was effected by calling me to the chair, and the appointment of Mr. C. C. McRae, of Chesterfield, as secretary.

I do not deem it necessary to say anything in regard to the proceedings of the meeting. A full and accurate record was kept of them at the time by the secretary, and was incorporated in his journal, which he sent to me, and is in my possession, and which is herewith presented as part of this narrative.

The following is a copy of it:

A meeting of citizens from different portions of the State of Virginia, convened at the Exchange Hotel, in the city of Richmond, on the 31st day of December, 1868, for the purpose of consultation in regard to matters explained in the narrative of their proceedings hereinafter supplied, was organized by inviting the Hon. A. H. H. Stuart to the chair, and by the appointment of C. C. McRae as secretary.

Mr. Stuart, on taking the chair, explained the objects for which the meeting was held, and the circumstances under and the manner in which it originated.

After considerable discussion, in which a large number of the meeting participated, and in which much harmony of feeling and views was displayed, it was determined that a committee of eight in number (of which the Hon. A. H. H. Stuart was made chairman by the meeting) should be appointed, charged with the duty of deliberating and reporting in regard to suitable business for the consideration of the meeting.

The Chair being requested to appoint the remaining members of the committee, accordingly named Messrs. George W. Bolling, of Petersburg; Thomas S. Flournoy, of Halifax; John L. Marye, Jr., of Fredericksburg; D. C. DeJarnette, of Caroline; Frank G. Ruffin, of Chesterfield; B. H. McGruder, of Albemarle; and James Johnston, of Bedford.

Whereupon, the meeting adjourned to convene on the ensuing evening at the same place.

According to the order of adjournment, the meeting again assembled on January 1st, 1869, when the committee appointed at the former session, through its chairman, submitted a report; the distinct features of which, being separately considered and acted on as a whole, after elaborate discussion was finally approved, with some modifications introduced by the action of the meeting by a vote nearly unanimous, only two gentlemen who participated in the meeting expressing unwillingness to concur in its final action. The names of several other gentlemen, who acted with the meeting, would doubtless have been added had they been present at the time of adjournment.

In the progress of the meeting, the following proceedings occurred: It was resolved that the Hon. Alexander H. H. Stuart be requested to serve as chairman of the committee of nine persons to be appointed to visit

Washington for the purpose indicated in another part of the proceedings, and that the Chair be requested to appoint a committee of three, to recommend for the consideration of the meeting the names of eight other gentlemen who, with the chairman, shall constitute the delegation referred to.

In accordance with the foregoing resolution, the Chair named Messrs. John Echols, F. G. Ruffin and James D. Johnston as the committee; who, after short retirement, reported, recommending as the delegation, in addition to the Hon. A. H. H. Stuart as chairman, Messrs. John L. Marye, Jr., of Fredericksburg; James F. Johnston, of Bedford; W. T. Sutherlin, of Danville; Wyndham Robertson, of Washington county; W. L. Owen, of Halifax; John B. Baldwin, of Augusta; James Neeson, of Richmond, and J. F. Slaughter, of Lynchburg.

The question being put on the recommendation of the committee, the same was unanimously approved.

It was resolved that the press of the city of Richmond be requested to publish these proceedings; and, on motion, the meeting adjourned.

C. C. McRae, *Secretary*.

The following is the report of the committee referred to, as modified by the meeting, with signatures thereto:

The undersigned, residents of different parts of Virginia, having, upon invitation of some of their own number, assembled in Richmond for the purpose of holding a conference in regard to the present imperilled condition of the Commonwealth, after a full interchange of opinions, have come to the following conclusions, which they respectfully submit to the calm and patriotic judgment of their countrymen:

1. While the convictions of the undersigned and, as they believe, of the people of Virginia generally remain unchanged, that the freedmen of the Southern States, in their present uneducated condition, are not prepared for the intelligent exercise of the elective franchise and the performance of other duties connected with public affairs, and are, therefore, at this time, unsafe depositaries of political power. Yet, in view of the verdict of public opinion in favor of their being allowed to exercise the right of suffrage as expressed in the recent elections, the undersigned are prepared, and they believe the majority of the people of Virginia are prepared, to surrender their opposition to its incorporation into their fundamental law as an offering on the altar of peace, and in the hope that union and harmony may be restored on the basis of universal suffrage and universal amnesty.

2. To give effect to this purpose, and to spare no effort to effect a speedy and permanent restoration of union and harmonious relations between the portions of our country which have for some years past been alienated, the undersigned will appoint a Committee of Nine from different parts of the State, and reflecting, as far as may be practicable, the public sentiment of the State, whose duty it shall be at an early day to proceed to Washington and be authorized to make known the views and purposes hereby declared to the Congress of the United States, and to take such other measures as they may think proper to aid in obtaining from that body such legislation

concerning the organic law of Virginia as Congress, in its wisdom, may deem expedient and best under all the circumstances. The delegation so to be constituted may fill vacancies, and are authorized to enlarge their number in their discretion.

3. The undersigned recommend to the people of Virginia, by primary meetings, to appoint delegates to a popular convention, to be held in Richmond on Wednesday, the 10th day of February, 1869, to receive the report of the committee appointed by this meeting, and to adopt such other measures as may be deemed most expedient to promote the objects herein indicated.

[Signed]

ALEX. H. H. STUART, Augusta.

THOMAS BRANCH, Richmond.

D. C. DeJARNETTE, Caroline.

THOMAS S. FLOURNOY, Halifax.

WYNDHAM ROBERTSON, Washington.

W. D. QUESENBERRY, Caroline.

B. H. MAGRUDER, Albemarle.

GEORGE W. BOLLING, Petersburg.

ASA D. DICKINSON, Prince Edward.

JOHN L. MARYE, JR., Fredericksburg.

W. C. KNIGHT, Richmond.

RO. WHITEHEAD, Nelson.

J. F. SLAUGHTER, Lynchburg.

A. G. PENDLETON, Giles.

J. D. JOHNSTON, Giles.

N. K. TROUT, Staunton.

H. M. BELL, Staunton.

JOHN ECHOLS, Staunton.

MATTHEW HARRISON, Loudoun.

FRANK G. RUFFIN, Chesterfield.

C. C. McRAE, Chesterfield.

R. L. WALKER, Chesterfield.

W. T. SUTHERLIN, Danville.

J. L. CARRINGTON, Richmond.

W. E. CAMERON, Petersburg.

J. F. JOHNSON, Liberty.

THOMAS J. MICHIE, Staunton.

JAMES NEESON, Richmond.

A correct copy,

C. C. McRAE, *Secretary.*

After the adjournment of the meeting on the 1st January, 1869, most of the members attended the public reception given by General Stoneman, the Federal general then in command in Richmond. He received them courteously, expressed sympathy with the objects of their meeting and hoped that it might prove successful.

Before leaving Richmond, I issued a summons to my associates on the "Committee of Nine" to assemble in Washington on the evening of the 8th January, 1869.

On the 2d of January, 1869, I returned to my home in Staunton. Within an hour or two after my arrival, Colonel Baldwin sent his servant to me with a request that I would let him know what we had done at the meeting in Richmond. As I was fatigued by my journey and, therefore, indisposed to write an account of our proceedings, I drew from my pocket a rough draft of the report of the committee of eight, of which I was chairman, and which, with a few immaterial alterations, had been adopted by the meeting, and handed it to the servant, with instructions to deliver it to Colonel Baldwin and say to him that it contained the substance of our action, and added that I would be obliged if Colonel Baldwin would return it to me as it was the only copy I had.

In a few hours the servant returned with the paper, and wrapped around it was the following note, written in pencil by the Colonel himself in his own familiar handwriting, and the original of which is filed with this narrative :

Dear Stuart :

I apprehend, from all I can learn from Bell, Trout and Echols, that you found rather a slim showing of sympathy at Richmond, and I shall not be surprised if you find the movement entirely tabooed before many days.

Our people seem to be in pretty much the same condition they were just before the fall of the Confederacy. Everybody looked for it and believed it was coming, and yet if any one dared to utter his thoughts he was set upon and cuffed without mercy.

Our people now do not seem to be prepared to discuss, or even to consider, any plan of dealing with the awful danger which threatens them, and I very much fear they will be caught as the people of old were by the deluge.

I am afraid of General Stoneman. They say he has no instructions from Washington, and yet he goes on to kick and cuff our people as if he were a very radical, aiming at political objects. Truly we are fallen on evil times, and I fear worse are coming.   Yours truly,

                                                                JOHN B. BALDWIN.

Sat. night.

I have thought proper to publish this letter, not only to vindicate the truth of history but to do justice to the memory of Colonel Baldwin. We were closely connected by the triple bond of blood, marriage and intimate personal friendship. His grandmother and my mother were sisters. His eldest sister was my wife. I had known him from his infancy, and when he commenced the practice of law, I invited him to become my partner in business, a relationship which continued for several years, and was terminated by mutual consent when he had attained eminence at the bar and we thought the interests of both would be promoted by a dissolution. We were in the habit of conferring and interchanging opinions on almost every public question that arose, and were generally in accord. Hence, we rarely failed to act in concert. He was one of the purest and most intellectual and bravest men, both physically and morally, I ever knew. If he had been at home when I wrote the article, " Senex," I have no doubt I would have conferred with him on the subject. But he was, as has already been stated, absent in Washington on professional business, and the date of his return was uncertain. I, therefore, wrote the article, " Senex," in his absence and without his knowledge. When he returned home, I was the first to make known to him what I had done, but as the newspapers containing " Senex " had not then been published he had had no opportunity of reading it. He concurred, generally, in the opinion that it was absolutely necessary to take some measures to arrest the passage by the Senate of the bill which had been passed by the House of Representatives, and, therefore, readily consented to attend the conference at my office on the morning of the 25th of December, and united in the invitation to other gentlemen to meet in Richmond on the 31st for consultation. But he was in nowise committed to any specific measures of policy.

On mature consideration, but after some hesitation, Colonel Baldwin finally decided to accept the position of member of "the Committee of Nine," to which he had been elected by the Richmond meeting. Having thus for the first time identified himself with the movement, he took hold of it with the grasp of a giant. He promptly made himself master of all the facts bearing on the various questions which were likely to come up for discussion before the Congressional committees. I venture to say that no member of the committee was so thoroughly equipped as he for the debates which were anticipated.

He was then in the prime of vigorous manhood, having just completed his forty-eighth year. He possessed a broad, luminous and well-cultivated intellect—powers of perception which, at times, vied in speed and brilliancy of action with flashes of electricity; a sound and clear judgment; masculine common sense, enlivened by ready and sparkling wit; an ample command of language; a wonderful power of elucidation by comparisons, which, though sometimes quaint and homely, were always apt and instructive. He was also thoroughly versed in the principles of constitutional law and popular rights.

Nature had been equally lavish to him in her physical gifts—of a large, well-proportioned and robust frame, and a massive head and spacious brow, on the scale of Daniel Webster's. His features were well-formed and expressive of every emotion. His voice, while not always melodious, was clear, distinct and penetrating, and thus could be heard by an audience of many thousands. His gesture, though not specially graceful and flowing, was, under all circumstances, striking and effective, and his elocution and intonations peculiarly adapted to make the desired impression on the crowds who thronged to hear him.

Knowing as I did that Colonel Baldwin possessed these great powers, I should have regarded myself as singularly neglectful of my duties as chairman of the Committee of Nine if I had failed to make them available in defence of the rights and interests of Virginia.

As chairman of the committee, it was my official duty to open the conferences with the Senate and House committees at Washington, by brief statements of the objects of our mission, and explanations of the features of the Underwood Constitution to which we objected, accompanied by some general remarks intended to present the matters in issue, and thus open the way for more full and thorough discussion. Having done this, it was my habit to ask leave to introduce Colonel Baldwin to present our views more at large. In the propriety of this course I am sure I was sustained by the unanimous judgment of the committee.

In this way a most important and responsible duty was confided to Colonel Baldwin, and I am sure every surviving member of the committee will bear willing testimony to the zeal, fidelity and ability with which he discharged it. He was also the author of a very strong paper, prepared at the request of the Judiciary Committee of the Senate, setting forth specifically and in detail the modifications of the Underwood Constitution which we wished to have made. This paper (which will be presently given) was signed by every member of the committee and placed in the hands of the Senate committee. In this way, Colonel Baldwin unquestionably became the most conspicuous member of the committee.

Begging pardon for this digression, which seemed to be necessary to correct misstatements which have been widely circulated, I resume the thread of my narrative.

In the interval between the adjournment of the Richmond meeting, on the 1st of January, 1869, and the assemblage of the " Committee of Nine " in Washington on the 8th of the same month, I took several steps intended to promote the success of our mission. The first of these was to address a letter to Hon. Horace Greeley, editor of New York *Tribune*, with whom I had, many years before, a pleasant personal acquaintance, informing him of the proceedings of the Richmond meeting, and of the appointment of the "Committee of Nine" to go to Washington and endeavor to secure a compromise of all our difficulties on the basis of " universal suffrage and universal amnesty," and asking him, if possible, to come to Washington and give us his assistance in accomplishing it.   I kept no copy of this letter, but its purport can readily be inferred from Mr. Greeley's reply, which was addressed to me at Washington, D. C.

The following is a copy of it, and the original will be filed with this paper:

"NEW YORK TRIBUNE," NEW YORK, *January 8, 1869.*

Dear Sir:

    I cannot be in Washington soon, nor is it essential. I shall try to make myself felt there without. I enclose my article on your mission, from last Monday's *Tribune,* though I presume you have already seen it.

    I beg you to confer directly with General Grant, and also with Senator Stewart, of Nevada, who is all right. I wish you would call on Senator Sumner, especially. He has faults of manner, not of purpose.

                            Yours,   HORACE GREELEY.

Hon. A. H. H. Stuart.

I was induced to write to Mr. Greeley because I was satisfied that, although he entertained many opinions in which I could not concur, he was a man of kind heart and honest purposes, as well as a jour-nalist of wonderful ability.

Mr. Greeley's letter, when read to the committee, gave us great encouragement, and he faithfully fulfilled his promise "to make himself felt" at Washington. His paper (the *Tribune*) contained, from day to day, leading articles in support of the objects of our mission, which had great effect in mollifying the prejudices and moulding the sentiment of members of Congress.

A day or two before leaving home to meet the committee in Washington, I received the following letter from Hon. John L. Marye, of Fredericksburg, who was a member of the committee:

FREDERICKSBURG, *Wednesday,* 6th Jan'y, 1868.

My Dear Sir:

    For reasons which I feel assured you would deem adequate (when stated to you) I am satisfied that our committee would be MATERIALLY aided by the presence and co-operation of Mr. George W. Bolling, of Petersburg. I write to suggest that you write to him and request him *to be* at Washington on Friday evening, and be ready to confer with us.

    Mr. Bolling has very favorable access to and footing with General Scho-field. The latter would *communicate* freely with *Mr. B.*

    It is almost certain that all of our committee will not be in attendance, and Mr. B. would be desirable as a substitute.

    I have had no intercourse with Mr. B. since our conference at Richmond, but am sure he would give us his help.

3

I am informed through intelligent sources that there is a gentleman at Norfolk, Mr. Gilbert C. Walker, who could help us in *some* of our *needs* there. He is a Northern man, but a resident of Norfolk, largely and influentially concerned in its commercial and financial affairs; a man of *integrity*, *intelligence, experience* in *public matters*, with *most favorable* personal relations and access to official personages, whose ear we should have. Mr. Walker has been a decided, out-spoken foe to the Underwood Constitution, and would act energetically and cordially in favor of our movement. I do not propose that *he* should be placed *on* the committee. But I am convinced that it would be well for you, in writing to Mr. Bolling, to ask Mr. B. to write to Mr. Walker *at once*, and request (as coming from Mr. Bolling) that he (Mr. W.) would be in Washington and extend his aid to us. I write it haste.

I am very truly yours,

Hon. A. H. H. Stuart.   JNO. L. MARYE.

On receiving this letter, I promptly wrote to Mr. Bolling, inviting him to meet the committee at Washington, and as I had no personal acquaintance with Mr. Gilbert C. Walker, I requested Mr. Bolling to give to Mr. Walker in my behalf a similar invitation. This I presume he did, as both Mr. Bolling and Mr. Walker came promptly to Washington, and announced their readiness to co-operate with the committee. It was in this way that Mr. Walker first became known to the people of Virginia and identified with her cause.

The first meeting of the committee was held at the National Hotel, in Washington city, on the evening of the 8th of January, 1869. On calling the roll, we were gratified to find that every member was present. Our proceedings were informal, and no record of them, in the form of a journal, was kept. All the members understood clearly the objects for which we had met, and the only matter which required consideration and discussion was the best means of accomplishing them. Many suggestions were made, which became the subject of conversation, and were adopted, modified or abandoned, according to the wishes of the majority. There were some propositions, however, which received unanimous approval : 1st. That the committee should meet daily, or oftener, for conference and interchange of ideas and information ; 2d. That we should invite the co-operation of Mr. Bolling, Mr. G. C. Walker, and his brother, Mr. Jonas Walker, and of all citizens of Virginia, who might be in Washington, in promoting the work of the committee; 3d. That we would, in a body, call on the President (Andrew Johnson) to pay our respects, but that as the close of his term of office was so near at hand, and his relations to Congress of such an unfriendly character, it would be useless to ask assistance from him ; 4th. That we would, without

delay, seek an interview with General Grant, the President elect, explain to him fully the grievances of which we complained, and earnestly
invoke his aid in relieving us from them ; 5th. That the members of
the committee, individually, and the gentlemen who proposed to co-
operate with them, should proceed, without delay, to seek conferences with the leading members of the two Houses of Congress, and
explain to them the objects of our mission, and impress upon them
the justice of our claims, and seek their aid in obtaining relief from
the dangers which threatened us.   ·

This programme was duly carried into effect. The committee, in
a body, called on President Johnson, and were courteously received
by him, but no effort was made to induce him to take any official
action in regard to the objects of our mission.

It is proper to state, that shortly after " the Committee of Nine "
assembled in Washington, two committees or delegations from Richmond made their appearance in Washington on behalf of the Republican party, one of them consisted, as we learned unofficially, of
Mr. Franklin Stearns, L. H. Chandler, William Forbes and Edgar
Allen, and probably others. The other, which was led by Governor
H. H. Wells, was more numerous, and composed of white and
colored men. The former, which consisted of men of intelligence,
education and good standing, was regarded as a Committee of *Ob-
servation*, and was supposed to be present, not with a view of making
factious opposition to every measure of relief which might be proposed by the Committee of Nine, but to see that nothing was done
prejudicial to the interests of the Conservative Republicans. The
Wells Committee, on the other hand, was emphatically a Committee
of *Obstruction* and *Antagonism*. It was in full sympathy with all
the test oaths, disfranchisements, and other objectionable features of
the Constitution, and opposed to any change in any of its provisions.

CONFERENCE WITH RECONSTRUCTION COMMITTEE OF HOUSE OF REPRESENTATIVES.

In accordance with the original programme, as above set forth, the
committee applied for and obtained permission to appear before the
Reconstruction Committee of the House of Representatives and the
Judiciary Committee of the Senate, to explain to them, respectively,
the grievances of which we complained and the nature of the redress
which we desired to obtain.

It is not necessary, for the purposes of this narrative, to give in detail all that occurred in the various interviews which were held by the Virginia committee with the committees of Congress. It is sufficient to mention some of the leading incidents which tend to show the varied phases of public opinion of that day, and to throw light on the motives and purposes of those who were prominent actors in them.

At the hour appointed for the conference with the Reconstruction Committee of the House of Representatives, all the members of the Committee of Nine were in attendance. We were politely received by ex-Governor Boutwell, chairman of the Committee, and after an interchange of salutations and introductions, we were assigned to the seats which had been provided for us. It then became my duty, as chairman of the committee, to open the interview by a brief explanation of the origin of our committee and the objects of our mission. Before I had concluded my remarks, we were interrupted by the arrival of the two Richmond committees, headed, respectively, by Mr. Franklin Stearns and Governor H. H. Wells, who expressed a wish to be present at the interview. This was readily granted with the assent of all parties. As the sessions of the Reconstruction Committee were necessarily short, being limited to the hour, 12 noon, appointed for the meeting of the House of Representatives, and as all parties desired to be heard in support of their respective opinions, the conference was continued by adjournment, from time to time, through several sessions of the Committee, during which full and free debate was allowed.

This discussion was conducted, on behalf of our committee, mainly by Colonel Baldwin. He had been speaker of the House of Delegates in the session of the General Assembly of Virginia, which had recently been held under the Peirpoint administration, and was, therefore, better posted than any other member of the committee in regard to its proceedings.

After he had presented, with great clearness and force, the views of the committee, Governor H. H. Wells took the floor as the representative of the opinions of the Radical Committee, of which he was chairman. As reported by Mr. Cowardin, of the *Dispatch*, he spoke substantially as follows: "Governor Wells said he did not believe that loyal men would be safe from wrong and outrage if the white people of Virginia were all enfranchised; he believed that the only mode of protecting them would be to adopt the Constitution made by the Underwood Convention *as it was;* he was satisfied that the adoption of the plan of the 'Committee of Nine' would break down the Republican party and destroy the last hope of ' Loyalists ' in Virginia. He was sure the people, whatever they might say now, would, in a few years, take away the rights of the negro unless the Republican party became strong enough to protect them, and the only way to secure strength to that party was to give it power to direct the restoration of the State ; none but the Republican party could secure justice to all classes and rebuild the State. There could be no justice, no education, no prosperity, save through the Republican party. That party would invite immigration, insure the safe investment of capital and put Virginia in the way of rapid improvement. He assured the Committee that there were ten millions of dollars ready, at this time, to be brought into the State under Republican auspices to build railroads, etc., etc. He declared that the new movement had not the support of Virginians; that he did not believe that ten thousand white people in Virginia would support it ; that if it is carried it would have to be carried by Republican votes, but the Republican party would not vote for it. They were opposed to reconstructing Virginia in that way. They would be willing to see the whites enfranchised after a few years when it could be done safely, but not now."

It was asked whether, if the plan of the " Nine " succeeded, the loyal men would have anything to compensate them for the concession that would be made. He replied, " None whatever."

The same reporter (Mr. Cowardin) says " Colonel Baldwin spoke eloquently for an hour in reply, and was listened to with marked attention. In reply to questions of the Committee, he expressed his confident belief that the people of the State would support and carry out in good faith the plan which he advocated."

By request of the committee, Mr. Franklin Stearns, of Richmond, a staunch Republican, and Chairman of the Conservative Republican Committee, addressed the Reconstruction Committee at some length, and said "that since the defeat of the Democratic party (meaning in the Presidential election of November, 1868,) the people of Virginia were ready to comply with the reconstruction laws, and more than half of the property holders were ready to restore the State on the basis proposed by the Committee of Nine. If the State was restored under the pending Constitution, with disfranchisements and county organizations stricken out, she would immediately have her prosperity revived, and rapidly grow in wealth and population. So restored, justice would be impartially administered, and all classes completely protected.

"Mr. Stearns condemned the 'Underwood Constitution,' and said it would be defeated by an *honest vote* of the people, but that its defeat would leave the State without a civil government, and subject to all the whims and caprices of military rule. Hence, as the representative of the Radical party of Virginia, he favored the programme of the Conservative Committee, which did offer the people some prospect of a stable government."

The reporter adds : "Mr. Stearns was listened to attentively, and his statement made a decided impression."

This synopsis of the discussion before the Reconstruction Committee of the House of Representatives will be sufficient to show the nature of the matters in issue, and the spirit in which they were presented by the several speakers.

CONFERENCES WITH JUDICIARY COMMITTEE OF SENATE.

The committee also had interviews with the Judiciary Committee of the Senate of an important and interesting character. But it is unnecessary to state the proceedings in detail. In all material matters they were similar to the proceedings before the Committee of Reconstruction of the House. This Committee was one of extraordinary ability. Among the members were Conkling, of New York, Frelinghuysen, of New Jersey, Doolittle, of Wisconsin, Trumbull, of Illinois, and others of almost equal celebrity. The conference having been opened by the Chairman of the Committee of Nine, by a brief statement of the objects of their mission, and of their objections to the Underwood Constitution, the further discussion of the subject was turned over to Colonel Baldwin, who made a clear and forcible exposition of the enormities contained in the Constitution. The Senators listened with great attention, and seemed to be desirous of making themselves acquainted with the subject. They asked many questions, which were promptly answered, giving the information that was sought. The interview was less formal than that with the House Committee, and the discussion of a more colloquial character, intended to promote a full and free interchange of facts and opinions, and the members manifested an earnest desire to acquire all the knowledge which was necessary to make them to act intelligently on the subject. Colonel Baldwin was the principal spokesman on behalf of Virginia, and presented the views of the committee with so much clearness and force as to leave a profound impression on the minds of the Senators. Before separating, the Senate Committee requested the Committee of Nine to prepare for their use, a condensed statement, in writing, of the grievances of which they complained, accompanied by a detailed draft of the amendments which they desired to have in-corporated into the Constitution. This was accordingly done a few days afterwards. The paper was prepared by Colonel Baldwin with great care, and after thorough scrutiny by the committee was, on 18th January, 1869, adopted and signed by every member of it, and sent to the Senate Committee. The full text of this paper was pub-lished, and is to be found in the columns of the newspapers of that day. It is as follows :

To the Judiciary Committee
of the United States Senate :

On behalf of the delegation of citizens of Virginia, and in accordance with the request of your committee, we beg leave respectfully to submit, in the form of amendments to House Bill 1485, now under your consideration, such modifications of the Constitution proposed by the late Convention as, in our opinion, will, under all the circumstances, lead to its acceptance by the people of Virginia.

It is due to candor to say, in this connection, that those who sent us here expressed, as we believe, the real feelings and purposes of the people of Virginia when they declared, " while the conviction of the undersigned and, as they believe, of the people of Virginia generally remains unchanged, that the freedmen of the Southern States, in their present uneducated condition, are not prepared for the intelligent exercise of the elective franchise and the performance of other duties connected with public affairs, and are therefore, at this time, unsafe depositaries of political power ; yet, in view of the ver-dict of public opinion in favor of their being allowed to exercise the right of suffrage, as expressed in the recent elections, the undersigned are pre-pared, and they believe the majority of the people of Virginia are prepared, to surrender their opposition to its incorporation into their fundamental law as an offering on the altar of peace, and in the hope that union and harmony may be restored on the basis of universal suffrage and universal amnesty."

Taking it, then, to be established as the policy of this government to require in Virginia a constitutional recognition and enforcement of the civil and political equality of all men before the law, we have, in the amendments proposed, inserted all the provisions looking to that result which Congress has heretofore deemed proper, and we have left undisturbed all the provi-sions of the proposed Constitution in any manner relating to that subject.

The first modification of the proposed Constitution suggested by us, is to strike from it all those features of disfranchisement and disqualification, and all those elements of bitterness and strife, political, sectional, and sectarian, which, in our judgment, are wholly incompatible with good government and good feeling, and tend to perpetuate alienations and discords, which all good citizens must deprecate. The power of a State to subject any of its citizens to disabilities for offences against the United States has been seriously ques-tioned. It seems to be conceded that for the purpose of the punishment no such power exists, and that disqualifications and disfranchisements are only admissible as measures of precaution and safety.

In this point of view, it is worthy of consideration that since the close of the war the people of Virginia have been living without disfranchisement or disability of any kind, under a government whose legislative and judicial departments and whose local organizations have been in the hands of the very classes whom it is sought by the proposed Constitution to exclude from every position of trust in the State. We claim, with confidence, that the result has been that the supremacy of law and order has been as fully maintained, and that the functions of good government have been as well performed, in Virginia as in any State in the Union.

It is believed that Article III, section one, paragraph four, would disfranchise not less than ten or fifteen thousand voters in the State, including all those whom the people have been accustomed to trust in public employments.

Article III, section seven, would disqualify for every position of public trust not less than ninety-five of every hundred of the white people of Virginia who would otherwise be eligible, and would, in connection with section three of the same Article, extend the like disability to serve upon juries.

It is believed that there is no advocate of universal negro suffrage who will not agree that in its application to Virginia at this time it is a fearful experiment, requiring for its success all the wisdom and experience that can be brought to its management ; and it is respectively submitted that to exclude from participation in State or local government at this time so large a proportion of those who, by experience in public affairs, are fitted to deal with this great problem, would be unwise and unsafe.

We earnestly declare that, in our belief, it would be wholly inconsistent with domestic tranquility, public order, or the security of the lives, liberty or property of the great body of the white population of Virginia.

The provision of Article XI, relating to church property, is an attempt to reverse the settled policy of Virginia, which restricts the ownership of church property in amount, and confines it strictly to the local religious congregation. The purpose is to enable "ecclesiastical bodies" outside of Virginia, in opposition to the legislation of the State, and against its judicial decisions, to take the churches of Virginia from the local congregations who built them. The provision opens a controversy, full of all the combined bitterness of party and section and sect, over every Presbyterian and Methodist church building in Virginia.

The next modification suggested by us is to strike from the proposed Constitution, and thus to leave to legislative enactment or modification, the whole of the cumbrous machinery for local organization, government and policy, which, in our judgment, is clearly unfitted to the condition of the State, and if fixed to the Constitution will be a cause of embarrassment and difficulty and strife, seriously affecting the public peace and the harmony and good order of society.

The population of Virginia is very sparsely and unequally distributed over the territory of the State, and the physical and geographical features of the country are such as to render wholly impracticable any arbitrary plan of subdivision for local purposes. The most we have been able to do thus far is to make the counties the units of local government, and to give to the county courts, composed of all the county justices, the control and direction of the local government and police.

In view of the introduction into our system of so large a political element so unequally distributed as to result in the complete predominance of the whole white race in one section of the State and of the colored race in another section, we are very earnestly of opinion that any system of local government and police engrafted upon the Constitution and placed under the absolute control of limited districts, will naturally incur the distrust and excite the apprehensions of the local minority and tend to collisions calculated to impair personal security and endanger the public peace.

The difficulties surrounding the subjects of local taxation and education, in regard to which we are satisfied that the proposed system will be found unequal and inefficient in its operation, and in its results intolerably expensive and oppressive.

The solution of these difficulties, which we propose, is to strike the whole of this system from the Constitution and leave it to the Legislature, in which all localities, interests and classes will be fully represented, to regulate the whole subject by laws which will be at all times open to modification and improvement, such as experience may suggest or the public interest may require.

The next modification proposed by us is to strike out the provisions in Article XI relating to homestead and other exemptions. The laws in Virginia now in force provide for homestead and other exemptions, prospective in their operation. The provisions of these laws are believed to be not materially different from those in the proposed Constitution, except in regard to past indebtedness, as to which we regard the proposed provision as clearly in conflict with the Constitution of the United States. The chief importance which we attach to striking out this provision grows out of its injurious effect upon the minds of the people, whose necessities already incline them to look with favor upon any suggestion of relief from pecuniary obligation.

The only remaining suggestion of modification is as to the maximum of taxation for local free school purposes in Article VIII, section 8.

It will be observed that we have made no objection to the school system proposed, except so far as it depends on the local organization, to which we have already referred.

No objection is offered in any quarter to the establishment of a thorough system of free public schools, at least as rapidly as the proposed Constitution requires; and although we have asked to strike out the *mode* of local taxation proposed, we have suggested a modification which avoids any diminution of the *amount* to be raised by taxation for public free school purposes.

In suggesting the modifications referred to, we by no means wish to be understood as conceding that the proposed Constitution is free from what we regard as important defects in other particulars, but we do not understand it to be the purpose of Congress to interfere in such matters further than may be required by high considerations affecting the integrity of the Constitution and the maintenance of justice and domestic tranquility. We have therefore confined our objections to provisions of the proposed Constitution, falling properly, as we believe, within the scope of such an inter-position.

The clauses which we ask to have stricken out from the proposed Constitution are of different degrees of importance, but the least important, we think, will be found to involve some grave public mischief or injustice. Those included in our first suggestion could not but plunge our State into civil anarchy and discord, and disturb the general and growing harmony of the two races of our people, if not to array them in deplorable hostility to one another. They would arrest immigration, paralyze all forms of industry, destroy our domestic peace and hope of prosperity, and render us a burden to the Union instead of an important addition to its resources, wealth, credit and power.

In our personal interview with the Committee, we called their attention to provisions of the proposed Constitution, and especially to that relating to usury, as instances of the insertion into a Constitution of matters peculiarly proper to be left to ordinary legislation, the provision in regard to usury is one new in Virginia, and will establish a policy which, whatever may be its merits, must seriously affect all the material interests of our people.

It is respectfully submitted, for the consideration of the Committee, whether a measure of legislation so important, and in regard to which opinion is so much divided, ought to be fixed in the Constitution and so placed beyond legislative control.

As to the mode of granting relief from the mischievous provisions to which we have referred—to-wit: by act of Congress, suggesting modifications as fundamental conditions precedent, we desire to say that it has been suggested as the result of an examination of the precedents found in the past legislation of Congress, and upon consultation with a number of the wisest and most experienced members of both Houses. In the preparation of the amendments proposed to the pending bill, we have endeavored fairly to follow the precedents established in like cases, and we may be permitted to suggest, in conclusion, that we believe it will be found that the modifications proposed by us will, in fact, conform the proposed Constitution to the principles and policy of the Reconstruction acts.

It is perhaps proper to say we, and those with whom we act, though concurring, as we believe, with the people of Virginia, do not claim to be authorized to speak for them.

Respectfully, your obedient servants,

ALEXANDER H. H. STUART,
JOHN B. BALDWIN,
WYNDHAM ROBERTSON,
W. T. SUTHERLIN,
JAMES NEESON,
J. F. JOHNSON,
W. L. OWEN,
J. L. MARYE, JR.,
J. F. SLAUGHTER,
Committee.

WASHINGTON CITY, January 18, 1869.

The following are the changes in the proposed Virginia Constitution, which the committee will ask Congress to enact:

House of Representatives, 1485.—Bill entitled "An act providing for an election in Virginia."

Amendments suggested for the consideration of the Senate Committee of the Judiciary:

First Amendment.—Strike out the whole of the first section after the enacting clause, and insert in lieu thereof three sections, as follows:

That the State of Virginia shall be entitled and admitted to representation in Congress as a State of the Union when the voters of the said State—who at the time of the election hereinafter provided for, shall be registered and qualified as such in compliance with the acts of Congress, known as the Reconstruction acts—shall have agreed to and ratified the Constitution adopted by the Convention which met in Richmond, Virginia, on the 3d day of December, Anno Domini, 1867, subject to and in accordance with the conditions and modifications hereinafter declared and proposed.

SECTION 2. *And be it further enacted,* That the foregoing section is subject to the following fundamental conditions precedent, and shall not take effect until the same and each of them are fully accepted by the voters of Virginia at the said election.

I. The Constitution of said State shall never be so amended or changed as to deprive any citizen or class of citizens of the United States of the right to vote in said State who are entitled to vote by the Constitution thereof herein recognized, except as a punishment for such crimes as are now felonies at common law, whereof they shall have been duly convicted under laws equally applicable to all the inhabitants of the State: *provided,* that any alteration of said Constitution may be made with regard to time and place of residence of voters.

II. That in the adoption and ratification of said Constitution there shall be omitted therefrom the following parts and provisions thereof, which, in the opinion of the Congress, are unnecessary for the protection of any right, and tend to retard and prevent the restoration of that harmony and good will among the people which are among the chief objects sought to be attained by the Reconstruction acts aforesaid, viz.:

1. The provision for disfranchisement and disqualification contained in Article III, section one, clause four, and in section seven of the same Article, and that relating to church property in Article XI of said Constitution.

2. The provision for local organization, government and police contained in Article VI, sections thirteen to twenty-one inclusive, those in Article VII and in the two last sentences of Article VIII, section eight.

3. The provision relating to homestead and other exemptions in Article XI, sections one to seven, inclusive.

III. That the limitations upon the power of taxation for public free school purposes in Article VIII, section eight, be changed from five mills to ten mills.

SECTION 3. *And be it further enacted,* That the said Constitution, subject to the said fundamental conditions, and with the modifications aforesaid, be submitted for ratification to the voters registered and qualified as aforesaid, according to the provisions of the Reconstruction acts, on the fourth Thurs-day of April, 1869. The vote on said Constitution shall be "for the Consti-tution, subject to the fundamental conditions prescribed by Congress," or "against the Constitution." The said election shall be held at the same places where the election for delegates to said convention was held, and under the regulations to be prescribed by the Commanding General of the military district and the returns made to him as directed by law.

Second Amendment.—Strike out in section five, line four, the word "Sep-tember," and insert "June."

Proposed Title.—"An act to provide for admitting the State of Virginia to representation in Congress."

CONFERENCES WITH GENERAL GRANT.

Very soon after their arrival in Washington, the committee took steps necessary to obtain an interview with General Grant, President-elect, who was then in the city awaiting his inauguration. With this end in view, the committee called on General Schofield, then acting Secretary of War, and, after explaining to him the objects of their mission, asked the favor of him to make known to General Grant their desire to call on him to pay their respects and have an oppor-tunity of explaining to him the objects of their visit to Washington. General Schofield, who expressed full sympathy with the objects we had in view, promptly agreed to do so. He accordingly called on General Grant, and made an arrangement with him to receive the committee on the 14th of January at a specified hour. About half an hour before the time indicated, the majority of the committee met in their room, with a view of going in a body to General Grant's headquarters. Unfortunately, however, in consequence of some misapprehension about the hour of meeting, two or three of the committee (of whom Colonel Baldwin was one) failed to attend. After waiting as long as they could, hoping the absent members would appear, the members present proceeded to the office of Gene-ral Schofield, who kindly agreed to accompany them to headquarters and introduce them to General Grant. The committee was received with frankness and courtesy by General Grant, who entered into general conversation with its members in a familiar way, which at once put every one at ease.

The committee, through their chairman, then proceeded to explain to him the objects of their visit to Washington. The objectionable features of the Underwood Constitution were fully explained to him, and also the disastrous consequences which would necessarily follow their adoption. General Grant gave close attention to all that was said, and showed, by the pertinent and searching questions which he asked from time to time, that he thoroughly understood and appreciated the injustice and oppression which would be done to the people of Virginia by adopting the Constitution without amendment.

The conversation then became of a more general character, in the course of which he did not hesitate to express in strong terms his opposition to the test-oaths and disfranchisements embodied in the Constitution. He referred, however, to the fact that, for the present, he was a mere military officer, and, as such, powerless to render any assistance. His language and manner throughout the interview left no doubt on the minds of the committee that if the Senate should fail to act on the bill then pending until after his inauguration, he would interpose in some way to afford relief. The interview lasted an hour or two, and the results were very gratifying to the committee.

When the committee returned to their hotel they found their associates, who had been disappointed in not attending the interview, much mortified at their mistake in regard to the time of holding it, which had prevented their participation in it.

During the next day rumors reached the committee that mischievous persons had represented to the friends of General Grant that the absence of the members, who had failed to attend the interview, was intentional and a premeditated mark of disrespect to General Grant. This absurd and malicious falsehood naturally created a strong feeling among all the members of the committee, and they at once determined to give the most emphatic contradiction to it, by seeking a second interview with General Grant, to enable every member of the committee to be present. A request to that effect was accordingly made, which was promptly granted.

At the time appointed for the second interview every member of the committee was present, and a number of distinguished gentlemen from Virginia, who had asked leave to accompany the committee. The whole party then proceeded in a body to General Grant's headquarters. They were cordially received, and the gentlemen of the committee, who had not been present at the former interview, were afforded an opportunity of explaining the mistake which had caused their absence, and their regret that they had been thereby denied the pleasure of participating in it.

The most interesting incident which I can recall in connection with this interview was the following : Shortly after all the gentlemen present had paid their respects to General Grant and been seated, he turned to the chairman of the committee, and, addressing him by name, said : " Mr. Stuart, since you were here the other day I have been thinking a good deal of the matters discussed in our interview, and looking somewhat into the provisions of your proposed Constitution ; and I must confess that, bad as the provisions in regard to test-oaths and disfranchisements unquestionably are, it seems to me that the county organization feature is, if possible, worse. In the eastern portion of your State the negro population is greatly in ex cess of the white. Under the county organization features of the new Constitution, as proposed, you must have in that section of the State negro judges, negro juries, negro magistrates, negro supervisors, and negro sheriffs and constables ; in other words, a negro government. Under such a condition of things, no decent white man can afford to live in that part of the State, and they will be compelled to move away. In the western part of the State, where the whites predominate, the condition of things will be reversed, and the negroes will have to remove. In this way the two races will be segregated by a geographical line, which is greatly to be deplored ; and what is more, the *labor* of the State will be separated from the *capital*, and the productive power of the State will be greatly impaired, if not destroyed." I believe I report the language of General Grant with almost absolutely literal accuracy. His sentiments, as well as the language in which he expressed them, made a profound impression on my mind at the time, and have remained fresh in my memory, because I have had frequent occasions to recall and repeat them in private conversations, from time to time, since they were first uttered.

A free talk between General Grant and the members of the committee then followed, in which he clearly indicated his sympathy with our movement, and his desire to see Virginia restored to the Union on fair and honorable terms. The interview was gratifying to every member of the committee, and they left him, cheered by the confident belief that at an early day after his inauguration, his strong arm would be interposed for the relief of Virginia.

INTERCOURSE OF MEMBERS OF THE COMMITTEE WITH SENATORS AND REPRESENTATIVES.

Immediately after the organization of the Committee of Nine in Washington, it was agreed that the members of the committee, singly or in pairs, should call on as many of the leading members of Congress as they could conveniently visit, either at the capitol or their lodgings.   Many other gentlemen from Virginia, who were in sympathy with the objects of the committee, were invited to co-operate with us in this important work.   Among those who were most efficient in this department of service, were Gilbert C. Walker, and his brother, Mr. Jonas Walker.   Being in some way connected by marriage with Senator Stewart, of Nevada, they had ready access to him, and at an early day secured his active assistance in promoting the objects of the committee.   Mr. Gilbert C. Walker, being a man of fine intel-lect, imposing appearance and manners, and a good talker, was well fitted to make a favorable impression on all classes of men.   Having been born and reared in the interior of New York, and being an avowed Republican in politics, he had no difficulty in approaching Northern Republicans and explaining to them the gross injustice and oppression which would be imposed on Virginia by the Underwood Constitution.   He devoted his whole time, for a week or ten days, to this good work, and reported the results of his labors, from time to time, to the committee.   They were deeply impressed with the value of his services in mitigating the asperity of party and sectional preju-dices, and awakening a more kindly sentiment in the minds of Northern men.   It was by work of this kind that Gilbert C. Walker won for himself the favorable regard of all Virginians who were then in Washington, and opened the way to the conspicuous position which he afterwards filled in Virginia.

CLOSING SCENES IN WASHINGTON.

After the lapse of ten days or more spent in earnest efforts to rescue Virginia from the ruin which threatened her, the committee felt that they had fulfilled the duties which had been entrusted to them. They had done all that they could hope to accomplish at that time. They had aroused the attention, not merely of Virginia and the Southern States, but of the whole North, to the enormities of the "Underwood Constitution."   They had secured, as advocates of jus-tice to Virginia, the New York *Tribune*, New York *Times*, Boston *Advertiser*, Chicago *Tribune*, and other leading organs of public opinion in the North and Northwest.   They had arrested the pas-sage of the House Bill in the Senate.   They had received satisfac-tory assurances from General Grant that—as soon as practicable after his inauguration as President—he would bring the subject to the attention of Congress, and endeavor to obtain for Virginia substantial relief.   In a word, the committee felt that they had faithfully tilled the political field and sown good seed, which, at the proper time, would germinate and bear an abundant harvest of blessings.   If the committee had been able to accomplish nothing more than the defeat by the Senate of the passage of the House Bill, submitting the Underwood Constitution without amendment for ratification, they would have felt that they had rendered a service of incalculable value to the State.

Let us pause a moment and contemplate the condition of things which existed when what was popularly called the "new movement" was set on foot.   The House Bill had been introduced and passed through all its stages by the House of Representatives without objection or debate.   This occurred a few days before Christmas recess of 1868, and the Bill was sent to the Senate for concurrence.   Parliamentary rules required (unless temporarily suspended) a reference to the Judiciary Committee, and a report from that Committee before the Bill could be put on its passage.   The delay thus caused prevented its passage by the Senate before the Christmas vacation.

No fair-minded man will venture to deny that, if *some responsible party* had not interposed objections to the Bill, it would have been taken up and passed by the Senate as it had been by the House, without debate.   The single question then submitted to the people of Virginia would have been the "ratification" or "rejection" of the Underwood Constitution which, in popular parlance, would have been a choice between "the devil and the deep sea."   If the Constitution were ratified, according to the estimate made by the "Committee of Nine" in their paper submitted to the Judiciary Committee of the Senate, NINETY-FIVE PER CENT. of the adult white population of Virginia would have been not only rendered *ineligible to any office*, but *deprived of the right of suffrage*, and rendered *incompetent to serve on a jury, civil or criminal !*

Under these circumstances, we would have had Wells for Governor, backed by a constituency consisting mainly of ignorant negroes and depraved whites.   The better class of white people would have been powerless.   We should have had, in the graphic language of General Grant, "negro judges, negro sheriffs, negro juries, negro magistrates —in a word, a negro government—which would have compelled every decent white man to move away !"

But this is not all.   Under such a condition of things, what was to prevent any emancipated slave from bringing suit against his late master to recover compensation for his service while he was held in slavery? Negro, or carpet-bag, judges would have been prompt to sustain such actions, and ignorant and interested juries eager to award verdicts for heavy damages. Each negro juryman would have had a personal interest in the question, as a verdict in one case would establish a precedent to enable him to maintain a similar suit against his former master! In this way, under the forms of law, the estate of every man, who had ever been a slave-holder, might have been confiscated!

If, on the other hand, the Constitution were "rejected," the people of Virginia would have been remitted to despotic military sway, with Wells, a mere dependent Governor, prepared to execute the arbitrary behests of the commander, for the time being, of Military District No. 1!

Nor could we have looked to Congress for relief! It would have been truly said we had contumaciously rejected a Constitution, to which we had refused to offer any objections, and which had been approved by the unanimous vote of both Houses of Congress!

There were some facts which had occurred in Richmond within the year 1868, the year preceding the visit of the "Committee of Nine" to Washington, which, while they did not seem to attract public attention at the time, were full of significance to every thoughtful observer.

Pierpoint had been recognized and regularly installed as Governor of Virginia in May, 1865. His administration had been as fair as the people of Virginia had a right to expect under the circumstances. A session of the Legislature was held while he occupied the Executive Mansion, and the Convention called to frame a Constitution met in Richmond on the 3d of December, 1867, and continued in session until about the 24th of April, 1868. The Constitution framed by this body provided for an election to be held on the 2d of June, 1868, to decide whether the Constitution should be "ratified" or "rejected," and at the same time that an election should be held for members of the General Assembly and for all State officers to be elected by the people under the Constitution.

It was further provided "that the returns of the election shall be made in duplicate, one copy to the Commanding General and one copy to the President of this Convention (Underwood), who shall give certificates of election to the persons elected"!

Almost simultaneously with the publication of the Constitution and of the election ordinance under it, a general order was issued

4

from military headquarters *removing Governor Pierpoint from office,*
and substituting Mr. H. H. Wells in his place! There was no
charge of official misconduct by Pierpoint, and his removal was,
obviously, for political reasons. He was too conservative to suit the
purposes of extreme partisans!

The Conservatives of Virginia, supposing that the election would
be held on the 2d of June, 1868, proceeded at once to organize for
the contest. A convention of the Conservatives was held in Richmond on the 4th of May, 1868, to nominate a State ticket to conduct
the canvass in opposition to the ratification of the Underwood Constitution and the election of H. H. Wells as Governor of Virginia.
At this convention, Colonel R. E. Withers was nominated for Governor, Hon. John L. Marye for Lieutenant-Governor, and General
James A. Walker for Attorney-General. These were gentlemen of
unquestionable ability and character, and each well qualified for the
high position for which he was nominated. These gentlemen without
delay took the field to canvass the State in opposition to the ratification of the Underwood Constitution. Wherever they appeared they
were met by enthusiastic crowds.

At that time (May, 1868,) neither the speakers nor the people of
Virginia could be led to believe that the intelligent population of the
North could be persuaded to tolerate universal suffrage among the
ignorant negroes of the South. Hence, the *disfranchisements* of the
whites and *enfranchisements* of the blacks, proposed by the Underwood Constitution, became subjects of the most unqualified denun-
ciations by the Conservative candidates and their advocates. It is
plain to see that one of the effects of this exciting popular canvass
was to stimulate and strengthen the public sentiment in *opposition to
negro suffrage,* and render more difficult the task of reconciling the
public mind of Virginia, a year later, to *acquiescence in it* even after
the announcement in the platform of the Republican party, in the
summer of 1868, of *universal negro suffrage* as one of their cardinal
doctrines. The people of Virginia still continued to hope against
hope, and it was not until the results of the Presidential and Congressional elections of 1868, which turned on that issue, had been
ascertained that their eyes were opened to the appalling and inevitable
fact that no reconstruction of civil government in the South was
possible which did not embody this hateful feature in it. No people
were ever called on to submit to a more painful sacrifice of feeling and
conviction. But, like the surrender of General Lee and his gallant
associates in arms, it was inevitable. Our great leaders were obliged

to submit to overwhelming force on the battlefield. The people of the South, in like manner, were constrained to surrender by an equally disastrous defeat in the field of political contest! The masses were in no condition to reason dispassionately. Indignation beclouded their judgment. This tends to explain why, at the outset, the movement of the "Committee of Nine," and the intelligent and patriotic citizens who co-operated with them, encountered such fierce opposition and reproach from a portion of the public press and some of the people.

During the pendency of the elections in the North in 1868, to which reference has been made, the elections in Virginia were postponed indefinitely to await the future action of Congress.

But the State ticket, which had been nominated on the 4th of May, 1868, eight months before, and under circumstances so entirely different, still retained their position as nominees, and, it was generally understood, that when an election should be ordered, H. H. Wells would be placed at the head of the opposing Radical ticket.

This glance at the condition of things that existed in Virginia at the time the "Committee of Nine" were in session in Washington, is necessary to make the narrative of subsequent events intelligible.

It has already been stated that very soon after the Committee of Nine assembled in Washington, two other committees, headed respectively by Mr. Franklin Stearns and Governor H. H. Wells, both professing to be Republican, appeared at Washington as representatives of the party in Richmond. It soon became manifest that the members of the first of these committees were essentially conservative, and in large measure sympathized with the general objects of the Committee of Nine. This discovery naturally broke down all barriers between these two committees, and thereafter they became allies, instead of adversaries, in the great work of liberating Virginia. Mr. George Rye also, who originally was a member of the Wells Committee, soon became satisfied that he occupied a false position, and became a zealous co-worker with the Stearns Committee, and rendered valuable assistance.

Community of purpose soon led to free interchange of sentiment and opinions, and while there were no formal interviews between the two committees as such, the individual members at an early day became acquainted with each other, and discussed, without reserve, the best means of promoting the objects they had in view.

In these conferences the future of Virginia was the subject of much earnest and anxious conversation, not merely with reference to the

probable action of the Government at Washington, but also as to the
best policy to be pursued to insure success in the elections that must
soon be ordered. All recognized the fact that Wells had been appointed military Governor with a view to give him *prestige* and pave
the way for his nomination as Governor at the coming State election.
All saw that, coming before the nominating convention under such
auspices, and backed by the whole power of the Radical Republicans,
Wells must prove a formidable candidate. Finally, all feared that,
let the popular vote as between Withers, a red-handed Confederate
colonel, and Wells, a loyal Republican, be as it might, Wells would
be "counted in."

These matters were informally, but fully and freely discussed by
individual members of the committees at Washington. It was suggested that possibly a condition of things might arise, in which the
conservative Republicans, who were co-operating with Mr. Stearns,
might hold the key to the political position! It might be found, on
consultation, in the event of the nomination of Wells, that it would
be unwise for the Conservative party to enter into the contest under
the leadership of Withers, and thereby encounter the double hazard
of his defeat by the popular vote, and the still greater one of his
being "*counted out*" by the returning officers!

It was known that the Republican Convention would be held at an
early day, and it was regarded as important that the leading conservative Republicans should be present at that meeting and endeavor to defeat the nomination of Wells. But if that should be
found impracticable, that they should withdraw and nominate some
safe conservative man, who would honestly and fairly administer the
duties of the office. In this connection, the names of Franklin
Stearns, William L. Owen, and Gilbert C. Walker were favorably
mentioned.

The primary object was the defeat of Wells—first, by preventing
his nomination in the Convention, and if that could not be done,
then by breaking the force of it by the nomination of a rival Republican candidate of conservative principles by the seceding members of the Convention. By adopting this course, the Conservative
party would be left free to decide, *at a later day*, whether it would be
best for them to continue the contest, under the lead of Withers,
Marye, and Walker, or to withdraw that ticket and give their support to the candidates named by the seceders from the Republican
Convention, and thereby consolidate all the conservative elements
in opposition to Wells. It is proper to add, however, that while

speculative opinions like these were freely expressed, no attempt was made to formulate or agree to any line of policy founded on them. Every one was left free to pursue in the future such course as his judgment might dictate.

After a sojourn of ten days or more in Washington, the members of the "Committee of Nine," believing that they had substantially accomplished the objects of their mission, returned to their respective homes, to await the development of the fruits of their labors.

Important events soon followed in rapid succession. General Grant was inaugurated on the 4th of March, 1869. The Republican Convention met at Petersburg on the 9th of the same month, and after a turbulent session of two days, nominated H. H. Wells for Governor, J. D. Harris (colored) for Lieutenant-Governor, and T. M. Bowden for Attorney-General.

But before these nominations were made, the conservative Republican members of the Convention, finding themselves overpowered by a riotous mob of ignorant negroes, led by unprincipled adventurers, withdrew from the Convention, and in a few days thereafter, aided by more than one hundred respectable gentlemen of both parties from other parts of the State, published an address to the people, nominating, in opposition to Wells and his associates, a Conservative-Republican ticket, composed of Gilbert C. Walker for Governor, John F. Lewis for Lieutenant-Governor, and James C. Taylor for Attorney-General. This address was signed by Franklin Stearns, Horace L. Kent, George Rye, John S. Develin, and about one hundred and fifty other gentlemen, whose names were known to the people of Virginia as men of intelligence and character, and largely interested in the welfare of the Commonwealth.

On the 7th of April, 1869, President Grant, in accordance with the assurances he had given to the "Committee of Nine," sent the following, which was his first message, to Congress :

WASHINGTON, D. C., *April 7th, 1869.*

To the Senate and
House of Representatives:

While I am aware that the time in which Congress proposes now to remain in session is very brief, and that it is its desire, so far as is consistent with the public interests, to avoid entering upon the general business of legislation, there is one subject which concerns so deeply the welfare of the country that I deem it my duty to bring it before you.

I have no doubt that you will concur with me in my opinion, that it is desirable to restore the States, which were engaged in the Rebellion, to their proper relations to the government and the country at as early a period as the people of those States shall be found willing to become peaceful and orderly communities, and to adopt and maintain such constitutions and laws as will effectually secure the civil and political rights of all persons within their borders.

The authority of the United States, which has been vindicated and established by its military power, must undoubtedly be asserted for the absolute protection of all its citizens in the full enjoyment of the freedom and security, which is the object of a republican government. But, whenever the people of a rebellious State are ready to enter, in good faith, upon the accomplishment of this object, in entire conformity with the constitutional authority of Congress, it is certainly desirable that all causes of irritation should be removed as promptly as possible, that a more perfect union may be established and the country be restored to peace and prosperity.

The Convention of the people of Virginia, which met in Richmond on Tuesday, December 3d, 1867, framed a Constitution for that State, which was adopted (endorsed) by the Convention on the 17th of April, 1868, and I desire respectfully to call the attention of Congress to the propriety of providing, by law, for the holding of an election in that State, at some time during the months of May and June next, under the direction of the military commander of the district, at which the question of the adoption of that Constitution shall be submitted to the citizens of the State; and, if this should seem desirable, I would recommend that a separate vote be taken on such parts as may be thought expedient, and that, at the same time and under the same authority, there shall be an election for the officers provided under such Constitution, and that the Constitution, or such parts thereof as shall have been adopted by the people, be submitted to Congress on the first Monday in December next for its consideration, so that, if the same is then approved, the necessary steps will have been taken for the restoration of the State of Virginia to its proper relations to the Union.

I am led to make this recommendation in the confident hope and belief that the people of that State are now ready to co-operate with the National Government in bringing it again into such relations to the Union as it ought, as soon as possible, to establish and maintain, and to give to all its people those equal rights, under the law, which were asserted in the Declaration of Independence, in the words of one of the most illustrious of its sons.

I desire, also, to ask the consideration of Congress to the question, whether there is not just ground for believing that the Constitution, framed by a convention of the people of Mississippi for that State, and once rejected, might not be again submitted to the people of that State in like manner and without the probability of the same result.

U. S. GRANT.

On the 10th of April, 1869, Congress responded to this message by passing a bill, the following synopsis of which is taken from the Code of Virginia of 1873, page 26:

The Act prescribed that the President of the United States may, at such time as he may deem best, submit the Constitution, which was framed by the

Convention, to the voters for ratification or rejection; and may also submit to a separate vote such provisions of said Constitution as he may deem best, such vote to be taken, either upon each of the said provisions alone, or in connection with the other portions, as he may direct.

That at the same time the members of the General Assembly and the officers of the State and members of Congress provided for by the Constitution shall be elected, and the Commanding General for the District of Virginia shall provide therefor.

That if the Constitution shall be ratified at such election, the Legislature of the State, elected as provided for, shall assemble in the Capitol of said State on the fourth Tuesday after the official promulgation of such ratification by the military officer commanding in the State.

That before the State of Virginia shall be admitted to representation in Congress, their several Legislatures, which may be hereafter lawfully organized, shall ratify the Fifteenth Amendment proposed by Congress to the Constitution of the United States, and then that all these proceedings shall be approved by Congress.   •

On the 14th of May, 1869, President Grant issued the following proclamation, under the authority given to him by the Act of Congress approved April 10th, 1869:

In pursuance of the provisions of the Act of Congress, approved April 10, 1869, I hereby designate the 6th day of July, 1869, as the time for submitting the Constitution, passed by the Convention which met in Richmond, Virginia, on Tuesday, the 3d day of December, 1867, to the voters of said State, registered at the date of such submission—viz.: July 6th, 1869—for ratification or rejection; and I submit, to a separate vote, the fourth clause of section 1, Article III, of said Constitution, which is in the following words:

"Every person who has been a Senator or Representative in Congress, or elector of President or Vice-President, or who held any office, civil or military, under the United States, or under any State, who, having previously taken an oath as a member of Congress, or as an officer of the United States, or as a member of any State Legislature, or as an executive or judicial officer of any State, shall have engaged in insurrection or rebellion against the same, or given aid or comfort to the enemies thereof."

This clause shall include the following officers: Governor, Lieutenant-Governor, Secretary of State, Auditor of Public Accounts, Second Auditor, Register of the Land Office, State Treasurer, Attorney-General, Sheriffs, Sergeants of a city or town, Commissioner of the Revenue, County Surveyors, Constables, Overseers of the Poor, Commissioner of the Board of Public Works, Judges of the Supreme Court, Judges of the Circuit Court, Judges of the Court of Hustings, Justices of the County Courts, Mayor, Recorder, Alderman, Councilman of a city or town, Coroners, Escheators, Inspectors of Tobacco, Flour, etc., Clerks of the Supreme, District, Circuit and County Courts, and of the Court of Hustings, and Attorneys for the Commonwealth: provided, that the Legislature may, by a vote of three-fifths of both Houses, remove the disabilities incurred by this clause, from any person included therein, by a separate vote in each case.

And I also submit to a separate vote section 7 of Article III of the said Constitution; which is in the following words :

" In addition to the foregoing oath of office, the Governor, Lieutenant-Governor, members of the General Assembly, Secretary of State, Auditor of Public Accounts, State Treasurer, Attorney-General, and all persons elected to any convention to frame a Constitution for this State, or to amend or revise this Constitution in any manner, and Mayor and Council of any city or town, shall, before they enter on the duties of their respective offices, take and subscribe the following oath or affirmation; provided, the disabilities therein contained may be individually removed by a three-fifths vote of the General Assembly : ' I, —————————, do solemnly swear (or affirm) that I have never voluntarily borne arms against the United States since I have been a citizen thereof; that I have voluntarily given no aid, countenance, counsel, or encouragement to persons engaged in armed hostility thereto; that I have never sought nor accepted, nor attempted to exercise, the functions of any office whatever under any authority or pretended authority in hostility to the United States; that I have not yielded a voluntary support to any pretended government, authority, power, or constitution within the United States hostile or inimical thereto. And I do further swear (or affirm) that, to the best of my knowledge and ability, I will support and defend the Constitution of the United States against all enemies, foreign and domestic; that I will bear true faith and allegiance to the same; that I take this obligation freely, without any mental reservation or purpose of evasion; and that I will well and faithfully discharge the duties of the office on which I am about to enter. So help me God.' The above oath shall also be taken by all the city and county officers before entering upon their duties, and by all other State officers not included in the above provision."

I direct the vote to be taken upon each of the above-cited provisions alone, and upon the other portions of the said Constitution in the following manner, viz., each voter favoring the ratification of the Constitution, excluding the provisions above quoted, as framed by the Convention of December 3d, 1867, shall express his judgment by voting for the Constitution. Each voter favoring the rejection of the Constitution, excluding the provisions above quoted, shall express his judgment by voting against the Constitution. Each voter will be allowed to cast a separate ballot for or against either or both of the provisions above quoted.

In testimony whereof, I have hereunto set my hand and caused the seal of the United States to be affixed.

Done at the city of Washington this 14th day of May, in the year of our Lord 1869, and of the Independence of the United States of America the ninety-third.

U. S. GRANT.

By the President :

HAMILTON FISH, *Secretary of State.*

It will be seen that this proclamation restricted the separate votes to be taken to the two clauses which imposed test-oaths and disfran-chisements, thus denying the right to a separate vote on the "county-organization," which he had, in the presence of the "Committee of Nine," emphatically denounced as the worst feature of the Consti-tution!

This singular and unexpected omission caused great surprise and a good deal of indignation, at the time, among the people of Virginia. The public press had made known to them the substance of what General Grant had said to the "Committee of Nine" in regard to this particular feature of the Constitution, and of the mischievous consequences which must inevitably follow its adoption. In the absence of all explanation, some were disposed to impute bad faith to President Grant. I did not concur in this view of the subject. I felt sure there must be some strong reason (which it would not be prudent to disclose at the time) which had constrained General Grant to forbear from including this clause among those upon which separate votes were to be taken.

And here, in justice to General Grant's memory, it is proper that I should say that, at a later day, I learned from an unquestionable source that I was right in my conjecture.

The question, as to what clauses should be voted on separately, was the subject of consideration in the Cabinet. There was little, if any, difference of opinion about the "test-oath" and the "disfranchise-ment" clauses. But when the "county-organization" clause came up, much diversity of thought developed itself. General Grant was earnestly in favor of submitting it separately, but a majority of the Cabinet had been led to believe that the secret but controlling reason why the people of Virginia wished to strike out that feature, was to rid themselves of the obligation to establish a system of free schools, with which it was so intimately blended. This view of the subject was pressed with so much warmth and earnestness that, although General Grant did not believe it to be true, he found himself obliged, for the sake of harmony in his Cabinet, to yield the point.

The President's proclamation became the subject of excited dis-cussion in the newspapers and on the street corners and at every place where half a dozen people met together. The disappointment was keenly felt, and the enquiry was on the lips of every intelligent man, "What shall we do?" This condition of things existed, not only among the younger and more impetuous classes; it prevailed, to a great extent, among the most judicious and thoughtful men of

the State.   In a word, the public mind *was unsettled* as to what was
the wisest course to pursue.

As an illustration of the condition of things which then existed, I
will refer to an incident within my own knowledge.

Business required my presence in Charlottesville, for a few days,
about the time of the issue of the President's proclamation.   As I
walked from the courthouse to the railroad depot, where I was to
take the cars on my return to my home in Staunton, I casually fell
in company with an old and valued friend, Professor John B. Minor,
one of the most honored professors of the University of Virginia,
who was also about to take the cars as far as the University of Virginia.
The President's proclamation naturally became the subject of discussion.   He inclined to the opinion that it would be best for the
people of Virginia to vote down the Underwood Constitution, and
said that such seemed to be the sentiment of his brother professors.
I differed with him, and we discussed the question until we arrived
at the University station, where the train then stopped for a few
moments.   As he was about leaving the train, he said to me he had
been impressed with some of the views I had presented, and begged
me, when I arrived at home, to write him a letter, giving more full
expression to them, which I promised to do.

On the following day I wrote a letter to him, giving my opinion in
regard to the proper policy to be pursued by the people of Virginia,
and some of the most urgent reasons in support of it.   This letter
was not written with any view to its publication.   But, in a day or
two afterwards, I received a note from Professor Minor, thanking me
for the letter, and stating, that as it had aided him and some of his
co-professors in coming to a right conclusion on the subject, he
thought it might possibly render a similar service to others, and he
had, therefore, taken the liberty, without asking my consent, to send
it to the Richmond *Enquirer* for publication.   It was, accordingly,
published in the *Enquirer*, and thence re-published in many other
papers.   The following is a copy of it:

LETTER ADDRESSED BY HON. ALEXANDER H. H. STUART TO PRO-
FESSOR JOHN B. MINOR.

STAUNTON, *May 24th, 1869.*

My Dear Sir:

When I casually met you a few days ago, you requested that
I would express to you, in writing, my views of the course the people of
Virginia should pursue in regard to the questions about to be submitted for
their decision under the President's proclamation.   I now proceed to do so.

There certainly was much disappointment felt when it was ascertained that the President had failed to include the "county organization" clauses of the Constitution among those which were to be submitted to the people to be voted on separately. It was known that the President had expressed strong opposition to these clauses, as tending to segregate the white and colored population by a geographical line, and to impair the productive power of the State, by separating the labor of the country from the capital of the Commonwealth. Hence a confident expectation was entertained that he would afford to the people an opportunity of striking these objectionable features from the proposed Constitution. In the first excitement occasioned by this disappointment, some persons expressed their purpose to try and defeat the whole instrument, by voting, first, to strike out the disfranchising clauses and the test-oath, and then against the instrument thus expurgated. This disposition was not unnatural under the circumstances. Within the four years which have elapsed since the close of the war the people of Virginia have been subjected to so much disappointment, annoyance, and obloquy, that they have become sensitive and in some degree soured.

But, unfortunately, we are in no condition now to take counsel of our wishes. We are not in that happy state in which we can afford to indulge in the luxury of a little *ill-temper*. We are bound by inexorable necessity to confront the stern realities of our situation, and to make the best we can of them. After giving to the subject the best consideration, I have satisfied myself that it is the true policy of the people of Virginia to vote to *strike out* the test-oath and disfranchising clauses, and then to vote *for the adoption* of the residue of the Constitution. I admit that it is a painful necessity, yet it is not the less a necessity.

It is true that we will not get *all* that we had expected to get, yet I think it is obvious that by so doing we gain a great deal. The Constitution, even when expurgated, will be a very objectionable instrument, but it is certainly much better than in its original form, and, in my judgment, it is infinitely preferable to *no Constitution at all.* We can at least live under it for a time, with the certain assurance that after awhile we can greatly improve it. It would tax my time and your patience too largely to give all the reasons which have brought my mind to this conclusion. But I will state one or two of the most prominent : It seems to me that in casting their votes under the President's proclamation, the people are called on to decide where the political power of the State is to rest hereafter, and who are to control her destinies in the future. They will have to elect between three competing propositions, neither of which is entirely acceptable, but there is no other open to us. These propositions are: 1st. To take the Underwood Constitution *pure and simple;* 2d. To vote the *whole Constitution down;* 3d. To adopt it, with the disfranchisement and test-oath stricken out. Let us now consider what is the practical bearing and effect of each one of these propositions. Let us see how it will affect the future *status* of the political power of the Commonwealth.

If we allow the Underwood Constitution to be adopted, with all of its disqualifications, it is obvious that we *voluntarily disfranchise ourselves* for a generation to come, and place the political power—the power to control our lives, liberty, and property—in the hands of the carpet-baggers and the worst classes of our own people. I presume there are few intelligent and upright men in the State who will favor this proposition, and I, therefore, pass it by without further commentary. Let us now consider the second. Suppose we vote the whole Constitution down, what follows? Some contend that matters would stand as they are. Assuming such to be the fact, I ask is that not bad enough? We would have Wells for our nominal Governor, and all of our offices filled by aliens and strangers. We would have justice administered under military supervision and by appointees of a military commandant. But what assurance have we that matters would remain as they are? How do we know whether our situation will not be rendered more intolerable than it is now? By voting down the Constitution altogether, we, in effect, recommit the whole political power of the State to a Radical Congress. Has the past action of that body been such as to render it desirable that they should again assume unlimited control over our destiny? I must acknowledge I think not. If we virtually decide that we will have nothing to do with shaping our fortunes, we compel Congress to take upon itself that office. The third proposition is, then, the only one that offers any hope of escape from the terrible evils by which we are threatened. If we strike out the restrictive features, and then adopt the residue of the instrument, while we do not gain all we want, we at least place the political power of the State in the hands of the better classes of the people of Virginia. We snatch it from the grasp of the carpet-baggers and their allies, and we withdraw it from the control of a Radical Congress. We will entitle ourselves to a restoration to our rights in the Union, and to the withdrawal of military supervision and control over us. We can elect officers and enact laws of our own, and within a year or two, after the excitement incident to these political struggles shall have passed away, we can call a new Convention and form a new Constitution adapted to our existing condition. By striking out the disfranchisements and test-oaths, almost the whole body of our population will be clothed with the power to vote and be rendered eligible to office. The principle of popular sovereignty will be established on a firm basis, and the voice of our own citizens will be potential in framing our future organic law and shaping our future policy.

I have thus stated, I think, fairly the three propositions between which the people of Virginia are compelled to choose. If there be any other open to them I am not aware of it. Ought the people of Virginia to hesitate between them? I think not. I think they ought to expurgate the Constitution and then adopt it. But it is all-important that we should spare no pains to secure a good Legislature and a good Governor. The reasons are too obvious to require enumeration. They will readily suggest themselves to every intelligent mind. If we expect good laws, we must elect a good Legislature. If we desire and wish an honest execution of the laws, we must choose a wise and honest Governor. And while this is at all times necessary, it is especially so now. The new Legislature will have to enact all laws necessary to put the new government into operation. The Constitution is not self-enforcing; it requires legislation to give effect to it. The new Governor will be clothed with the *veto power* to check hasty and im-

provident legislation.   Need I say anything to show to the people the necessity of making a wise selection of those who are to wield powers, fraught
with so much of weal or woe to the State?

Very truly yours, etc.,

ALEX. H. H. STUART.

But, resuming the narrative of events in their chronological order,
it will be observed that the withdrawal of the anti-Wells wing of the
Republican party from the Convention of the party at Petersburg,
and their subsequent nomination of a State ticket of Conservative-
Republicans, put a new face on the condition of public affairs.   There
were now three distinct State tickets in the field.   First, the Withers
ticket, which represented the Conservative party, which was opposed
to the general policy of the Republican party and to the Underwood
Constitution ; second, the Wells ticket, which was in favor of the
harshest policy of the Republican party and of the Underwood Constitution just as it came from the hands of the Convention, without
any amendment; and, third, the Walker ticket, which, while on national
questions it agreed with the conservative branch of the Republican
party, was earnestly and inflexibly opposed to the adoption of the
Underwood Constitution, unless some of its most objectionable features were stricken out.   The contest, therefore, seemed as if it
would assume a tripartite character, involving so many and such
complicated questions as to render it difficult for the masses of the
people to know what to think or how to act !

Under these circumstances, the executive committee, which had
been appointed by the popular Convention of May 4th, 1868 (which
had nominated Withers and his associates), deemed it wise to call a
new Convention, to meet in Richmond on the 28th April, 1869, to
consider and decide what course it would be best to pursue, under
the new condition of affairs, to enable all opponents of the unmodi-
fied Underwood Constitution, without sacrifice of principle, to act in
harmony.

The Convention accordingly assembled in Richmond on the 28th
April, 1869, and immediately after its organization, Messrs. Withers,
Marye and Walker, with a view to relieve the Convention from any
embarrassment arising out of their nominations, made by the Convention of 4th of May, 1868, patriotically resigned their respective
claims to said nominations.   The Convention was thus left free to act,
as if no such nominations had ever been made, and with an eye single
to what was best for the safety and welfare of the State, under existing circumstances.

The whole subject, in all its aspects, was fully and ably discussed by gentlemen whose names and public services gave ample assurance of their patriotic purposes ; and, after mature deliberation, the convention finally decided—

1st. That the resignations of Messrs. Withers, Marye and Walker be accepted.

2d. That it was not expedient to make *any nominations* to fill their places ; but, "while expressing its hostility to the leading and general features of the Constitution, and recognizing the necessity of organization for the purpose of defeating such provisions as may be submitted separately," declined to make any recommendation to the Conservative voters of the State as to their suffrages upon the Constitution, expurgated of said provisions, or as to the candidates that may be before the people, feeling well assured that their own good sense and patriotism will lead them to such results as will best subserve the true and substantial interests of the Commonwealth."

These resolutions were adopted on 28th April, 1869, two weeks before it was known what provisions of the Constitution would be submitted for separate votes. The proclamation of President Grant, indicating them, was not issued until 14th May, 1869.

The practical effect of the action of the Convention was, to leave but *two State tickets* in the field, and to narrow and simplify the issue to be decided by the people to a choice between Wells & Co. and the original Underwood Constitution, on the one hand, or Walker and his associates and the Constitution, stripped of its most objectionable features, on the other.

This action of the Convention was hailed with great enthusiasm by the people of Virginia, as it gave them almost certain assurance of relief from the horrors of the Underwood Constitution and the domination of Wells!

Both parties immediately set to work to organize for the contest, by selecting candidates for the Senate and House of Delegates and all other offices which were to be filled at the coming election ; and notwithstanding the disappointment caused by the failure of President Grant in his proclamation to allow separate votes in regard to other objectionable features of the Constitution, there was little, if any, relaxation in the effort to arouse the people to a proper sense of the dangers which threatened them, and to stimulate them to vigorous efforts to ward them off.

The canvass was prosecuted with great spirit. The candidates entered the field in person, and traversed the State, making speeches to the crowds assembled at the court-houses and other public places. Gilbert C. Walker, being a man of imposing appearance and a good speaker, and being introduced and endorsed by Conservative gentlemen, was received with enthusiasm as the champion of the rights of the people. From these exhibitions of public opinion it seemed manifest that the combined Conservative party would certainly achieve a brilliant victory, unless some unexpected obstacle should be interposed by Federal authority to impede its onward progress.

Thus matters stood until about the 20th of June, 1869. On that day I received a telegram from Mr. Raleigh T. Daniel and Messrs. Branch and Fisher, his associates on the Executive Committee, urging me to come to Richmond as promptly as possible on business of an urgent character I replied to this communication that I would go to Richmond the next day, and could be found at the residence of Dr. Hunter McGuire, who then lived diagonally across Broad street from Ford's Hotel. I accordingly went to Richmond, and within a few minutes after my arrival at Dr. McGuire's, the gentlemen above named called on me and explained the objects of their summons. They said they had learned from an authentic source that General Canby, then in command of the United States troops at Richmond, had expressed the opinion *that under the terms of the Reconstruction acts it would become his duty to prevent any member-elect of the Legislature from taking his seat unless he would take the oath prescribed by the act of July 2d, 1862, commonly called the " iron-clad oath," and that he proposed to issue a military order to that effect !*

It was obvious that the results of such a measure would be disastrous to the interests of the Conservative party, in destroying confidence and unseating a large number of the members who would probably be elected to the Legislature. It might also tend to arouse a feeling of indignation among the people, that might endanger the success of the Conservative ticket and defeat the expurgation and ratification of the Constitution.

The object of the gentlemen in summoning me to Richmond was to confer with me as to the best means of defeating the plans of General Canby, and to invite me to render such assistance as I could in accomplishing that object.

I remained the following day in Richmond in conference with the committee, and after obtaining a copy of General Grant's telegram to General Meade, commander of the troops in Georgia, dated 2d March, 1868, I told them I could not see that I could render any service by remaining longer, but would return home and endeavor to devise some means of extricating the State from the dangers which threatened her. Accordingly I came home the following day.

On my return, after careful consideration, I prepared the following letter to General Grant :

STAUNTON, *June 25th, 1869.*

To His Excellency,
    the President of the United States:

SIR,—I respectfully beg leave to bring to your notice a matter which deeply affects the people of Virginia, and which, in my judgment, calls for Executive interposition.

You are doubtless aware of the fact that the 6th day of July has been named as the day for the election of State officers under the new Constitution, which is submitted, at the same time, for ratification or rejection, under the terms of the Reconstruction acts of Congress, and your orders made in pursuance thereof.

The people of Virginia, recognizing the considerate regard which you have displayed for their interests and feelings, in affording them the opportunity of expurgating the proposed Constitution of two of its most obnoxious features, have determined, in good faith, to accept the residue of the Constitution and, in all respects, to comply with the terms prescribed by the acts of Congress and your proclamation.

With this view, they have proceeded to make nominations of a State ticket and members of the Legislature, taking care, in all cases, to nominate none who were ineligible under the provisions of the Fourteenth Amendment of the Constitution of the United States.

Within a few days past, however, a rumor has become prevalent, which I have reason to believe well founded, that General Canby, the military commander of Virginia, has expressed the opinion that, under the terms of the Reconstruction acts, it would become his duty to prevent any member elect of the Legislature from taking his seat, unless he would take the oath prescribed by the act of July 2d, 1862, commonly called the "iron-clad" oath.

While no one questions the good faith and upright purposes of General Canby, I am persuaded that he has placed an erroneous construction on the 9th clause of the act of July 19th, 1867.

In this position I am sustained by very high judicial authority, to whom, within a few days past, the question has been informally submitted, and also, as I believe, by your telegram to General Meade, on 2d March, 1868, in regard to the officers elected, under similar circumstances, in Georgia. That telegram is in the following words: "The officers elected under the new Constitution of Georgia are not officers of the provisional government referred to in the Reconstruction acts, nor are they officers elected under any so-called State authority, and are not, therefore, required to take the oath prescribed in section 9, act of July 19, 1867. The eligibility to hold office must be determined by the new Constitution and the amendment to the United States Constitution, designated as Article XIV."

The language of the 9th section of the act of July 19th, 1867, is, I believe, substantially as follows: "That all members of said boards of registration and all persons hereafter elected or appointed under any so-called State or municipal authority, or by detail or appointment of the district commander, shall be required to take and to subscribe the oath of office prescribed by law for officers of the United States."

I respectfully submit that this act of Congress refers to the existing government of the State of Virginia, which exists only by sufferance and is properly styled a "so-called government." In the contemplation of Congress, it is a government not lawfully established, and in no sense a government *de jure*. It is simply a temporary, provisional and "so called" government.

But I respectfully submit, with equal confidence, that the new government, now in process of establishment in Virginia under the direct authority of Congress, is in nowise a "so-called" government, but, at each step of its progress, is a lawful, *de jure* government, and that the reservation of power by Congress to examine and approve the Constitution, does not make it either a provisional or "so-called" government.

In support of this position, I respectfully refer to the fact that Congress obviously contemplated action by the Legislature, so elected, on the proposed Fifteenth Amendment of the Constitution. It can hardly be supposed that Congress would authorize the Legislature of a mere "so-called" government to exercise one of the highest functions of a *de jure* government, viz.: to vote for or against an amendment of the Constitution of the United States.

I also respectfully refer to the 6th section of the act of Congress under which the election in Virginia is about to be held. That section provides "That in either of said States, the commanding general, subject to the approval of the President of the United States, may suspend, until the action of the Legislatures elected under their Constitutions, respectively, all laws that he may deem unjust and oppressive to the people."

Here it will be seen that the power to suspend injurious laws is expressly limited "until the action of the Legislatures elected under their Constitutions, respectively."

Why is this dispensing power given at all, and why is it subjected to the limitation imposed? Clearly it is given because the present government is a mere "so-called" government, whose action is subordinate to military authority, while, on the other hand, it is limited, because the Legislature elected under the new Constitution is a Legislature recognized as *de jure* and competent to enact the laws necessary for the welfare of the people. When that Legislature meets, the suspending power of the military commander ceases. The civil power is re-established on a lawful basis, which is recognized by Congress, in advance, as superseding the necessity for military intervention.

I would further respectfully suggest that the interpretation given by General Canby to the acts of Congress is directly at variance with the policy recommended by the Executive, sanctioned by Congress, and which is now being carried out under your proclamation, directing separate votes to be taken on the test-oath and disfranchising clauses of the Constitution.

It was obviously the purpose of Congress and the Executive to afford to the people of Virginia an opportunity of excluding those objectionable features from the Constitution. But, assuming General Canby's construction to be correct, of what avail would a unanimous vote to exclude those clauses be, if, in spite of such vote, the very test-oaths and disfranchisements thus stricken from the instrument shall be applied to all officers elected under the expurgated Constitution? The practical result would be that, while these objectionable clauses would be stricken out by the vote of the people on the 6th of July, they would be reinstated by military authority, on the assembling of the Legislature, four weeks after the adoption of the Constitution.

I respectfully submit that no such condition of things could have been contemplated either by Congress or the Executive.

I need hardly add anything in regard to the inexpediency of the course which seems to be contemplated by General Canby. The people of Virginia are sincerely desirous of seeing harmony and good feeling restored. They have surrendered many cherished convictions to secure this result. But now, when we are on the eve of its accomplishment, a new and fearful element of discord and ill-feeling is about being introduced, which, if persisted in, will entail lasting evils on our country.

For these and other reasons, which I will not trouble you by stating in detail, I now most respectfully, on behalf of the people of Virginia, request that you will cause such instructions to be given to General Canby as may lead him to conform his action to your telegram to General Meade, above quoted, and thus avert the mischiefs which would otherwise result to the State of Virginia.

Having for the last six months used every effort in my power to secure the restoration of my native State to her proper relations to the Federal Government, I have felt it to be a solemn duty to make this appeal to you to so exercise the prerogative of your high office as to secure the prompt accomplishment of that most desirable result.

Very respectfully, your obedient servant,

ALEX. H. H. STUART.

After the letter had been written and a fair copy made, by a confidential friend, many difficulties presented themselves as to the best means of ensuring its safe delivery to President Grant. I felt that if I entrusted it to the mail, it was very doubtful whether General Grant would ever see or hear of it. While my thoughts were thus occupied, I fortunately saw my old and valued friend, Hon. John F. Lewis, passing my office. I immediately invited him in and explained to him the object of my recent visit to Richmond and the danger by which we were threatened. I also read to him the letter to Grant, which I had prepared and explained to him the necessity of having it promptly and safely delivered into the President's own hands, and proposed, that as he was a personal and political friend of the President and could readily gain access to him, he should go to Washington and deliver the letter. This he readily agreed to do. I then placed the fair copy of the letter in an unsealed envelope, and after directing it to President Grant, I suggested that it would be well for him, before calling on General Grant, to read the letter to General Rawlins. then acting Secretary of War, and try to secure his co-operation with us.

On the following day, which I think was the 26th of June, 1869, Mr. Lewis went to Washington and was absent for several days. On his return, he informed me that he had had an interview with General Rawlins and read to him my letter to the President, and that General Rawlins had expressed, in emphatic terms, his concurrence in the views expressed in it, and his readiness to do anything in his power to secure the revocation of General Canby's order. Mr. Lewis added that he had then sealed the letter and delivered it, in person, to the President, who, after reading it, said he would give the subject his attention without delay. But he gave no intimation as to what his action would be. Of course, no personal answer to that letter was expected; but the official response was awaited with intense anxiety, as much of weal or woe to the Commonwealth hung upon it. In a few days, the response came in the most acceptable form in which it could have been presented, viz.: a peremptory mandate to General Canby to rescind his general order.

This mandate was promptly obeyed, and thus, by the vigorous and patriotic interposition of General Grant, the last obstacle to the deliverance of Virginia from tyrannical misrule was removed. The spirits of the people were revived ; the canvass was prosecuted with renewed vigor and energy. Finally, on the 6th of July, 1869, a glorious victory was won by the Conservatives. The Underwood Constitution was expurgated of its test-oath and disfranchisements and adopted ; Gilbert C. Walker and his associates were elected to fill the high offices for which they had respectively been nominated, and a Legislature chosen which reflected the sentiment of the people. Virginia was thus practically restored to her place in the Union and her citizens reinvested with all the rights of freemen! In a word, the great work for which the Committee of Nine and their associates had labored so faithfully and energetically for six months, in the face of the storm of misrepresentation and obloquy by which they had been assailed, was finished, and the committee were able to retire from the field of action with the proud consciousness that the results had fully demonstrated the wisdom and patriotism of their conduct.

I cannot close this "Narrative" without bearing my willing and grateful testimony to the patriotic and magnanimous conduct of General Grant toward the people of Virginia in all their troubles. He received their representatives with kindness and affability, and extended to them all the courtesy which was due to them as gentlemen. He listened to all their complaints with patience and close attention, and met every appeal in behalf of justice to Virginia in a spirit of fairness and generosity. I believed in 1869 that he was disposed to make every concession in the interests of peace which he could make consistently with his obligations to the party which had chosen him as its representative. He was the head and front of a great party flushed with victory and still laboring under the excitement of the recent fierce conflicts of the war. As such he was necessarily a party man. But he was more. He was a patriot, and in the eloquent language of the late Hon. William C. Rives, he never ceased "to remember that he had a country to serve as well as a party to obey"!

ADDENDUM TO THE FOREGOING NARRATIVE.

—

After taking leave of General Grant in January, 1869, in Washington, I had no opportunity of meeting him again personally until 25th of June, 1872.

In October, 1871, a vacancy having been created in the Board of Directors of the Trustees of the Peabody Education Fund by the death of Admiral Farragut, one of the original trustees appointed by Mr. Peabody, I was elected by the surviving members of the Board to succeed him in the administration of this beneficent and honorable trust.

At the next succeeding meeting of the Board, which was held in Boston on the 25th of June, 1872, I took my seat for the first time as a member of the body of which General Grant was also a member. In this way we were brought into close association at almost all the meetings of the Board which were held from 1872 to 1884 inclusive. During all this lapse of years, while there was nothing like intimacy between us, our relations were uniformly those of courtesy and good feeling.

When General Grant closed his earthly career on the 23d of July, 1885, the whole country was filled with sympathy and sorrow and mourning, which were shared in full measure by his late associate members of the Peabody Board.

In anticipation of the next ensuing annual meeting of the Board, which was appointed to be held in New York on the 7th day of October, 1885, I received a note from Hon. Robert C. Winthrop, President of the Board, informing me that he understood it to be the wish of many of the friends of General Grant that I should prepare and offer the formal tribute to his memory and character, to be entered on the records of the Board.

I must acknowledge that this indication of myself to perform this delicate and important duty was entirely unexpected, for I had supposed it would have been devolved on ex-Secretary of State Hon. Hamilton Fish, Hon. William M. Evarts, or the late Chief Justice, Morrison R. Waite, who were also members of the Board, and whose personal and political relations to General Grant had been of a much more intimate character than mine. But I undertook the duty with pleasure, because it afforded me, the only representative of Virginia on the Board, a suitable and welcome opportunity of speaking in such terms as I deemed proper in commemoration of the talents, public services, virtues, and catholic patriotism of the illustrious deceased, and more especially of the signal assistance which he had given to my native State on more than one occasion of her sorest need.

In pursuance of this arrangement, when the President, the Hon. Robert C. Winthrop, had closed his address with an eloquent and touching reference to the death of General Grant, I addressed the Board as follows:

"MR. CHAIRMAN,—I hope I shall not be regarded by my colleagues as officious or obtrusive in moving that so much of our chairman's address as refers to the death of General Grant be referred to a select committee of three, to consider and report what action should be taken by the Board in relation thereto.

General Grant, though a native and resident of the North, in fact belonged to the whole country, and it has seemed to me that it would tend to give emphasis to that fact if the movement to do honor to his memory were to come from a Southern man.

I, therefore, as the representative of Virginia—a State which was under many obligations to General Grant—take the liberty of submitting that motion."

The motion was passed, and Messrs. Stuart, Hayes and Manning were appointed the committee.

On the following morning I submitted the paper, which I had prepared for the consideration of the committee, and it was promptly and unanimously approved by them without modification or amendment, and I was instructed to report it to the Board. The following is the minute touching this report:

Mr. Stuart, in behalf of the committee to consider the tribute paid to General Grant, submitted the following report and resolutions, which were unanimously adopted, all the members rising when the question was put:

The committee to whom was referred so much of our chairman's opening address as refers to the death of General U. S. Grant have had the same under consideration, and respectfully submit the following

REPORT.

Death has again broken the ranks of our Board. General Ulysses S. Grant, the laurel-crowned warrior, the statesman who was twice elevated by the suffrages of the American people to the Presidency of the United States, the large-hearted patriot whose affections and aspirations during life were dedicated to his country's welfare and honor, the soldier who fought through long years of war that peace and all its attendant blessings might be secured to his countrymen, has been summoned from our side.

He went to his grave honored and lamented by men of all sections, and parties, and races. Men who had been arrayed against him on the battlefield twenty years ago were no less sincere in their grief for his death than those who had stood by his side in the deadly encounters of war. All appreciated his patriotic purposes—all admired his heroic courage and steadfastness—all honored his truthfulness and fidelity to every obligation. Bold, fearless, and aggressive in war, he was humane and magnanimous in the hour of victory. When mainly through his efforts civil war had ceased, he was among the first to seek to calm the angry passions to which it had given birth, and to invoke the blessings of peace and the restoration of union in fact as well as in name.

All remember how his patriotic appeal to his countrymen at the commencement of his first Presidential term, "Let us have peace," thrilled the heart of every true American from the Lakes to the Gulf, and from the Atlantic to the Pacific. From that hour to the close of his earthly career there is good reason to believe that the first wish of his heart was to witness the fulfilment of that prayer. When he stood, as it were, on the verge of the grave—when his mortal frame was wasted by disease, and his *tongue* had lost the power of giving utterance to the thoughts which filled his great soul—he made the *hand* which had so successfully wielded the sword in defence of the Union its substitute, to record his gratitude to God for having permitted him to live long enough to witness the restoration of union and fraternity between his lately discordant countrymen.

These noble sentiments sank deeply into the American mind, and awakened an echo in every patriotic heart. When he was stricken with the disease, which finally proved fatal, the hearts of the people of all sections overflowed with sympathy, and when the end came, a wail of grief was heard throughout our whole country, which found expression in popular meetings, through the public press, and in every other mode of testifying respect and affection known to civilized society, and his obsequies were celebrated with a solemn pomp and ceremony unparalleled in our country since the death of Washington.

General Grant was one of the sixteen original trustees named by Mr. Peabody himself to administer his beneficent trust in behalf of the illiterate children of the Southern States. He was in full sympathy with the purpose of the founder of the trust, and earnestly and cordially co-operated with his associates in their efforts to fulfil it.

At the date of his appointment, he was, with probably one exception, the youngest member of the Board, and his robust frame and apparently vigorous health gave promise of long life. But as it has pleased Him, in whose hands are the issues of life and death, to order otherwise, all that remains for us is, with bowed heads and reverent hearts, to submit to His decree.

Having assembled now at our annual meeting for the first time since this great affliction fell upon us, we, the surviving members of the Board of Trustees of the Peabody Educational Fund, gladly embrace the opportunity to place on our official records this testimonial of our profound esteem for the character of our deceased associate, of our sincere grief at his loss, and of our sympathy with his widow and family in their bereavement. ·

Of the achievements of General Grant, as a soldier and a statesman, we have purposely forborne to speak more fully. They are of too recent date, and in some respects too closely connected with the political and party contests of the day to admit of impartial judgment by contemporaries. We therefore remit these subjects to the domain of history, to which they properly belong.

But there are aspects of his character and attributes of his nature which elevate him far above the plane of the mere politician.   Upon these all can dwell with pleasure. His heroic courage, his unselfish devotion to his country, his fidelity to his friends, and his magnanimity to those who had been his enemies, his prompt obedience to every call of duty, and his broad and catholic patriotism, which embraced in its scope his whole country, and ignored all sectional divisions, must command the approval of all good men. Like Washington, he believed "the union of the States " to be " the palladium of our political safety and prosperity," and no one was more prompt than he "to frown upon the first dawning of every attempt to alienate any portion of our country from the rest, or to enfeeble the sacred ties which now link together the various parts."

Whatever differences of opinion may exist as to the wisdom of special acts, which he felt called on to perform during his long and brilliant career, few will be found disposed to question the purity of his motives, and a still smaller number to deny his title to be regarded as one of the most illustrious men of the nineteenth century.

In private life he was faithful in the discharge of every duty.   A devoted husband, an affectionate and indulgent father, a law-abiding citizen, a kind neighbor, a courteous and affable gentleman, he enjoyed the confidence and esteem of all who knew him, and few had warmer and more steadfast and devoted friends.

As a member of this Board, he was prompt in his attendance on its sessions, and an active and zealous supporter of every measure proposed by it for the promotion of the sacred trusts committed to its charge, and the surviving members will never cease to deplore the loss of his companionship and the withdrawal of the moral weight and influence which his great name gave to the deliberations and action of the Board.

RESOLUTIONS.

Resolved, That the foregoing report be approved and adopted by the Board, and that it be spread at large on our record as a heartfelt though imperfect tribute of affection and respect by the surviving members of the Board to the memory of their late distinguished associate.

Resolved, That our Chairman be requested to transmit a properly authenticated copy of these proceedings to the widow and family of General Grant, with an assurance of the profound sympathy of each and every member of the Board in their sore bereavement.